Stratford-upon-Avon
Second Series

General Editor: Jeremy Hav

Professor of Modern British Literature,
University of Trondheim, Norway

The British Working-Class Novel in the Twentieth Century

Editor: Jeremy Hawthorn

Edward Arnold

© Edward Arnold (Publishers) Ltd 1984

First published in Great Britain 1984 by
Edward Arnold (Publishers) Ltd, 41 Bedford Square, London WC1B 3DQ

Edward Arnold (Australia) Pty Ltd, 80 Waverley Road, Caulfield East,
 Victoria 3145, Australia

Edward Arnold, 300 North Charles Street, Baltimore, Maryland 21201, USA

British Library Cataloguing in Publication Data

The British working-class novel in the
 twentieth century.—(Stratford-upon-Avon
 studies. Second series)
 1. English literature—20th century—
 History and criticism   2. Laboring class
 writings, English—History and criticism
 I. Hawthorn, Jeremy   II. Series
 823'.912'09920623   PR478.L3

ISBN 0-7131-6415-8

Text set in 10/11 pt Garamond Compugraphic
by Colset Private Ltd, Singapore
Printed and bound in Great Britain by
Biddles Ltd, Guildford and King's Lynn

Contents

Acknowledgments

The editor and publishers gratefully acknowledge help received from the Pantyfedwen Fund of St David's University College, Lampeter. A generous grant from the fund has made it possible to include four pages of photographs in this volume.

The publishers would like to thank the following for permission to include copyright material:

W.H. Allen & Co. for extracts from Alan Sillitoe: *Loneliness of the Long Distance Runner, Saturday Night and Sunday Morning, Key to the Door, Death of William Posters, Men Women and Children, The Storyteller, The Ragman's Daughter, A Start in Life* and *Tree on Fire*; Jonathan Cape Ltd and the Estate of Walter Greenwood for extracts from Walter Greenwood: *Love on the Dole*; Curtis Brown Limited on behalf of the Estate of James Leslie Mitchell for extracts from Lewis Grassic Gibbon: *A Scots Quair*, copyright 1946 by Ray Mitchell; Frank Graham Publishers and Mrs S Magill for extracts from Jack Common: *Kiddar's Luck*; Lawrence & Wishart Ltd for extracts from Robert Tressell: *The Ragged Trousered Philanthropist* and Tessa Sayle for extracts from Alan Sillitoe: *Key to the Door, Death of William Posters, Men Women and Children, The Storyteller, The Ragman's Daughter, A Start in Life* and *Tree on Fire*.

Preface

For some people, 'working-class novel' is a contradiction in terms. C.C. Barfoot, commenting upon a book concerned with the portrayal of youth in post-war British working-class fiction, observes that nothing 'that is said about Jack Common, Brendan Behan, Alan Sillitoe or Barry Hines here disguises the fact that to shape a fiction, however unconventionally, and however loyal the writer may remain to the people who bore and sustained him, is an act that produces a result that is not in itself compatible with working class aspirations.'[1]

The complaint is not unfamiliar. We have been told that the very form of the novel is 'bourgeois', that (as Barfoot argues) there is a conflict between the interest that the novel takes in the individuality of its characters and their predicaments, and the working-class sources of its material. Moreover, the 'realism' favoured by working-class novelists has, in recent years, been treated with extreme suspicion by certain sections of the Left, and others have suggested that nothing acceptable to a middle-class or commercial publisher can possibly be at all in the interests of working-class people.

The trouble with all of these arguments is not that they are false but that they are half – or perhaps quarter – truths. The novel as literary genre *does* have an intimate relationship with the middle class, both in terms of its historical emergence and also of its continuing sociology: its readership and conditions of production. Sitting alone in a study wrestling with words is very unlike the working experience of a manual worker in a car factory and much more like the working experience of, say, an accountant. Becoming a writer *can* cut someone from the working class off from his or her roots, a point made by David Craig in his essay in this collection concerned with Alan Sillitoe, and by Michael Pickering and Kevin Robins in their essay on Jack Common. This may explain why many working-class writers write more about family experiences than the actual work process, as Ruth Sherry suggests is true of Irish writers in particular.

[1]C.C. Barfoot, 'Current Literature 1982', *English Studies* 64.6 (1983), p. 545, He is commenting on Ronald Paul, *Fire in Our Hearts*, (Acta Universitatis Gothoburgensis, 1982).

And such things as literacy, leisure time for reading, publishers sympathetic to their values (not to mention teachers and lecturers), have all been much more easily obtained by upper- and middle-class people than by members of the working class.

But it would be a serious mistake to assume that such things were therefore 'middle-class'. (On that line of arguing we would have to assume that decent housing was 'middle-class'.) The struggle of the organized working class for universal education, public libraries, their own publishing outlets and – not least – adequate leisure time, gives the lie to that assumption.

Moreover, it is crucial to stress both that the working-class novel has roots in the working class, and also that its very nature is transformed as a result of its appropriation by the class. As illustration of the former point we can cite Sid Chaplin's comments on his debt to the tradition of oral story-telling in this volume. And Peter Miles's contribution shows that modes of novel-reading native to the working class – word-of-mouth recommendation, reading groups, shared copies of novels, workplace study circles, trade-union libraries – constitute more than an alternative channel of distribution: they involve new manners of apprehension. To read a novel in a break at work along with your workmates is to read differently from the way a privileged person in a private study reads – and academics had better remember this.

It is not just the ostensible friends of the working class on the Left who have denied the existence of the working-class novel; as a number of writers in this collection of essays point out, with the revealing exception of Lawrence few if any of the writers examined in this volume find a place in official syllabuses in schools or universities. I read Grassic Gibbon, Tressell, Greenwood and the others *after* completing a degree in English literature. . . . As Graham Holderness argues in his essay, the texts concerned urgently need to be reprinted and 'educationally mobilized'. (And not just the texts of novels. In 1982 Stephen Spender was able approvingly to quote Blake Morrison to the effect that Tony Harrison was 'the first genuine working-class poet England has produced'.[2] No doubt Harrison himself might be happy to suggest a course of reading to correct such a view.)

Sid Chaplin talks of the effort to 'give people a voice', a phrase that calls Tillie Olsen to mind. Tillie Olsen was concerned with different 'silenced' people, people rendered mute by their colour, gender, or class. Ruth Sherry points out in her essay that there is no Irish Tillie Olsen, and we can go further and regret that none of the writers under consideration in this volume are women. Paradoxically, though, Sid Chaplin reveals that as a young man he looked upon writing as a 'feminine' activity. Perhaps this type-casting of the role of the writer explains why a number of the contributors to this volume comment positively on the way in which some working-class novelists portray female life and experience. Michael

[2]Stephen Spender, review of Tony Harrison, *The School of Eloquence. New York Review of Books* (15 July 1982). Blake Morrison's comment is to be found in the *London Review of Books* (1–14 April 1982).

Pickering and Kevin Robins make this point with reference to Jack Common's investigation into 'gender identity', and Deirdre Burton finds much to praise in Grassic Gibbon's treatment of women's cultural experience. Moreover, Ruth Sherry advances some very interesting possible explanations for the fact that Irish men wrote with considerable understanding of working women.

Highlighting another sort of 'silence', Peter Keating has referred tellingly to a comment by Henry James in his Preface to *The Princess Casamassima*: 'the figures in any picture, the agents in any drama, are interesting only in proportion as they feel their respective situations.'[3] James is explicit that 'our care and sympathy care comparatively little for what happens to the stupid, the coarse and the blind; care for it and for the effects of it, at the most as helping to precipitate what happens to the more deeply wondering, to the really sentient.' The brutality behind the urbanity is chilling, but it also relies on certain assumptions – most notably that working-class people (implied if not stated by James) are not articulate. This touches on some modern debates – around the research of Basil Bernstein and William Labov, for example. Without getting too deeply embroiled in these we can note that it is true both that some members of the working-class are extremely articulate, and also that forms of articulacy, self-expression and self-analysis are developed with education and that where educational facilities are poor or non-existent then these associated qualities may be in restricted supply.

According to Peter Keating the whole history of the attempts by generations of writers to present the working classes in fiction is concerned with the problem of how to write about (in James's words) 'the muffled, the faint, the just sufficient, the barely intelligent'. Or, in the words of Alan Sillitoe as quoted by David Craig, 'Emotions have to be delineated in the minds of people who are not usually prone to describing them.'

Is this, as C.C. Barfoot seems to suggest, a surrender to un-working-class individualism? I think not. An interest in a character's individuality or subjectivity is not incompatible with an interest in the character as representative of the class. Middle-class critics have been rather too fond in recent years of explaining to working-class people how many of their values, aspirations and ideals are 'bourgeois'. As Roger Webster shows in his essay on *Love on the Dole*, a novel repeatedly criticized in these terms can be read in a far more productive way and seen as a much more complex text than such attacks presume.

This is not to say that 'class' is no problem for a novelist from the working class; it clearly is. Graham Martin's essay on Lawrence provides further evidence that the adequate investigation of such a complex topic required all the talent and ability of a very talented and able novelist.

We hope that the present collection of essays will bring the work of many unjustly neglected novelists to the attention of new readers. But if all it succeeds in doing is establishing a rival canon, or providing a convenient

[3]P. J. Keating, *The Working Classes in Victorian Fiction* (London, Routledge and Kegan Paul, 1971), p. 47.

syllabus list, it will not have met our expectations. As Tony Davies's essay insists, we need to redefine and consolidate the past in the present. By changing our view of the past of our literature, let us start to alter our conception of its present. And by so doing, let us alter our own present and our future.

Jeremy Hawthorn

Note

Robert Noonan (author, as 'Robert Tressell', of *The Ragged Trousered Philanthropists*) was probably born in Dublin in 1870. By 1902, after a period in South Africa, he was house-painting in Hastings. He died in Liverpool in 1911 and was buried in a pauper's grave. His novel first appeared in abridged form in 1914. A restored text was published in 1955 (London, Lawrence and Wishart) and since 1965 has been available, introduced by Alan Sillitoe, in Granada paperback.

F. C. Ball's biographical researches culminated in *One of the Damned: The Life and Times of Robert Tressell* (London, Weidenfeld and Nicolson, 1973). J. B. Mitchell explores the novel in *Robert Tressell and 'The Ragged Trousered Philanthropists'* (London, Lawrence and Wishart, 1969), and the Robert Tressell Workshop assembles miscellaneous studies (with a useful glossary and index) in *The Robert Tressell Papers* (Rochester, WEA, 1982). M. Eagleton and D. Pierce's *Attitudes to Class in the English Novel* (London, Thames and Hudson, 1979) contains a brief discussion. F. Swinnerton's *The Adventures of a Manuscript: Being the Story of 'The Ragged Trousered Philanthropists'* (London, Richards, 1956) is of slight interest. D. Smith devotes a valuable chapter to the novel in his *Socialist Propaganda in the Twentieth-Century British Novel* (London, Macmillan, 1978), and J. B. Mitchell contributes 'Early Harvest: Three Anti-Capitalist Novels Published in 1914' to H. G. Klaus, ed., *The Socialist Novel in Britain* (Brighton, Harvester, 1982).

R. Williams discusses the novel in his foreword to Mitchell's *Tressell* and in 'The Robert Tressell Memorial Lecture, 1982', *History Workshop Journal* 16 (1983), pp. 74–82. Other articles of interest on the novel include: J. Beeching, '*The Ragged Trousered Philanthropists*', *Our Time* VII (1948), pp. 196–9, and 'The Uncensoring of *The Ragged Trousered Philanthropists*', *Marxist Quarterly* II (1955), pp. 217–19; D. Craig, 'The Growth of Modern Fiction', *Marxism Today* (November, 1961), pp. 346–9; J. G. Kennedy's somewhat tortuous 'Voynich, Bennett and Tressell: Two Alternatives for Realism in the Transition Age', *English Literature in Transition* XIII (1970), pp. 254–86; B. Mayne, '*The Ragged Trousered Philanthropists*: An Appraisal of an Edwardian Novel of Social Protest', *Twentieth-Century Literature* XIII (1967), pp. 73–83; J. B. Mitchell, '*The Ragged Trousered Philanthropists*: Cornerstone of a Proletarian Literary Culture and of Socialist Realism in English Literature', *Zeitschrift für Anglistik und Amerikanistik* X (1962), pp. 33–55; P. Nazareth, 'A Committed Novel', *Transition* (Kampala) VI (1967), pp. 35–40; J. Nettleton, 'Robert Tressell and the Liverpool Connection', *HWJ* 12 (1981), pp. 163–71; C. Woolf, 'A Masterpiece Restored', *Aylesford Review* II (1958), pp. 149–57. 'Talking to Kathleen Tressell' appeared in *Labour Monthly* L (1968), pp. 261–3.

1

The Painter's Bible and the British Workman: Robert Tressell's Literary Activism

Peter Miles

The Ragged Trousered Philanthropists has no place in the received academic literary canon.[1] In 1973 Tressell's biographer could remark that 'Oxford and Cambridge [literary] historians have never heard of the book'.[2] Tressell's novel of Hastings working-class life has subsequently continued to serve as familiar reference-point for cultural analysts and social and socialist historians,[3] but sheer enthusiasts have probably done as much to keep the book before a reading public as the schools of traditional criticism and literary history. Certainly Tressell has been identified as one of the two or three working-class writers attracting 'serious regard' on literature courses, but that observation was designed less to acknowledge sustained attention to Tressell in academic constructions of 'Edwardian' writing than to highlight even greater effacement of such later writers as Brierley, Boden, Coombes and Lewis Jones.[4] Unequivocally opposed to a system denying leisure, culture and the benefits of civilization to the majority, and with his distinctly un-Jamesian approach to writing fiction, Tressell has proved a prickly candidate for admittance to the pantheon of English Literature, or even for mandarin patronage as 'one of our uneducated poets' 'sleeping nameless in their scattered graves'. His book's survival without such supports consequently encourages enquiry into the conditions and strengths of the life of *The Ragged Trousered Philanthropists* within a broadly based model of British culture and of readers' interaction with texts. Exploring the mode of existence of the book within such models illuminates how the text has provided conditions for readers' co-operation in its adversarial stance towards dominant

[1] Page-references in parenthesis are to the Lawrence and Wishart edition.
[2] F. C. Ball, *One of the Damned: The Life and Times of Robert Tressell* (London, Weidenfeld and Nicolson, 1973), p. 186.
[3] E.g., S. Meacham, *A Life Apart: The English Working Class 1890–1914* (London, Thames and Hudson, 1977); C. Nicolson, 'Edwardian England and the Coming of the First World War' in A. O'Day, ed., *The Edwardian Age: Conflict and Stability* (London, Macmillan, 1979), pp. 144–68; D. Kynaston, *King Labour: The British Working Class 1850–1914* (London, Allen and Unwin, 1976).
[4] C. Snee, 'Working Class Literature or Proletarian Writing?' in J. Clark *et al.*, eds., *Culture and Crisis in Britain in the Thirties* (London, Lawrence and Wishart, 1979), p. 190.

social, political and cultural structures.

Tressell's book does, however, enjoy a history outside the academy. Marked by familiarity, affection and enthusiasm, this history comprises recorded anecdote and the still living, though socially delimited cultural consciousness fostering such anecdotes. From this communal perception it is evident that continued reading of Tressell owes much to a popular tradition of interpersonal recommendation and dissemination, largely at the grass roots of the British labour movement. Unlike normative transactions over the bookseller's counter, this tradition of transmission possesses, or has been endowed with, qualities of intimacy and engagement. These reinforce the character of the tradition as the expression of an active desire that others should share the experience of the book and contribute to the furthering of its educative function.

As far as it is recorded at all, this history registers typical moments and contexts of discovery and transmission. Tom Thomas, for example, is not unusual in first personally encountering the book through a political meeting:

> Seeking the real cause of that ghastly blood bath [the Great War], I heard of meetings at Finsbury Park on Sunday mornings. At these, which were organised by the *Herald* League, I listened to anti-war speakers who sometimes received quite a rough handling from some of the crowd. Here I bought the *New Leader*, the paper of the Independent Labour Party, and other literature and learned how the war, in their opinion, was caused. It was here that I bought my first copy of *The Ragged Trousered Philanthropists* which was to me as to many others both a revelation and an inspiration.[5]

Thomas was 'inspired' to dramatize the book, and the fact of that adaptation, first performed by the Hackney People's Players in 1927, constitutes an evident expression of that desire to extend transmission, to expand the audience from lone novel-reader to a 'sociable' community of witnesses, which is a typical and identifiable element of readers' interaction with this particular text.[6] Thomas's adaptation had influence beyond its initial performances, for the play's success has been recognized as the principal foundation of the Workers' Theatre Movement's efforts in propaganda drama through the early 1930s.[7] Published twice in the interwar period, Thomas's adaptation stimulated and enabled performances of *The Ragged Trousered Philanthropists* by other groups.[8] Another adaptation, by Frank

[5]T. Thomas, 'A Propertyless Theatre for the Propertyless Class', *History Workshop Journal* 4 (1977), p. 114.

[6]Ball, *Life*, pp. 213–16; R. Samuel, 'Documents and Texts from the Workers' Theatre Movement (1928–1936): Editorial Introduction', *HWJ* 4 (1977), pp. 103–12; Thomas, 'Theatre', pp. 117–18; L. A. Jones, 'The Workers' Theatre in the Thirties', *Marxism Today* XVIII (1974), pp. 271–80.

[7]A. van Gyseghem, 'British Theatre in the Thirties: An Autobiographical Record', in Clark, *Culture*, p. 212.

[8]T. Thomas, *The Ragged Trousered Philanthropists: A Play in Four Acts and Seven Scenes*

Rhodes, was played after the Second World War by the Unity Mobile Theatre Players, and, as I write, a further adaptation, by Stephen Lowe, goes into production at the Half Moon theatre.[9] Dramatic versions of the novel and of Tressell's life were televised in 1967 and 1983.

Bert Hogenkamp recalls that in 1934 200 copies of the novel were sold on site following a building strike in Putney. A member of the Workers' Film and Photo League sought to increase the modes of dissemination of the book by filming it, using the same site as set.[10] A little earlier Eric Blair discovered the book, not directly through his voracious reading, but thanks to the recommendation of a friendly Leeds branch-librarian.[11] Though doubting that a proletarian literature could develop within a bourgeois culture, Orwell firmly broadcast his opinion that *The Ragged Trousered Philanthropists* had always seemed to him 'a wonderful book'.[12] Alan Sillitoe has recalled having the book passed on to him while with the RAF in Malaya, the donor recommending it as the book which won the 1945 election for Labour.[13] Testimony to encountering the book within particular contexts of transmission still continues, as John Nettleton, a shop-steward, demonstrates:

> I first heard it when I was on a ship. These few pages ['The Great Money Trick'] are still done at branch meetings and they are still done in what they call the 'hut' at building sites whenever they're rained off, because it is as relevant today as the day he wrote it. I know lads who have got that off by heart. And every new apprentice who ever comes on the building site on the Liverpool Cathedral, that's his first lesson. And he learns that before he learns about the trade; he learns that, and that's the way it should be.
> . . . . Among the painters of Merseyside, as everywhere else, it is universally read, but also by other sections of the working class; and it's used extensively on on-site meetings and in study-groups.[14]

It is certainly not trivial that the physical transfer of the book, the lending or giving of copies, is integral to the book's mode of existence – even to its myth. Besides Tressell's, one gathers, 'there cannot be many serious novels which frequently change hands on building sites, in factories and among

. . . based on the novel of the same name by Robert Tressall [sic] (London, Richards, 1936); this was a revised printing of the Labour Publishing Company edition of 1928.
[9]Ball, *Life*, p. 215; S. Lowe, *The Ragged Trousered Philanthropists, based on the book by Robert Tressell* (London, Methuen, 1983).
[10]B. Hogenkamp, 'Making Films with a Purpose: Film-Making and the Working Class', in Clark, *Culture*, pp. 263–5.
[11]B. Crick, *George Orwell: A Life*, revised edition (London, Secker and Warburg, 1981), p. 137.
[12]G. Orwell and D. Hawkins, 'The Proletarian Writer', in S. Orwell and I. Angus, eds., *The Collected Essays, Journalism and Letters of George Orwell* (4 vols., London, Secker and Warburg, 1968) II, p. 39.
[13]A. Sillitoe, *Mountains and Caverns* (London, W. H. Allen, 1975), p. 145.
[14]J. Nettleton, 'Robert Tressell and the Liverpool Connection', *HWJ* 12 (1981), pp. 164, 170.

trades unionists'.[15] Particular copies are often described as 'tattered' or 'well-thumbed', implying not only how thoroughly and often the book has been read, but by how many readers. A 1955 reviewer declared that among the troops in Burma it was 'handed around and read and reread until it literally fell to pieces'.[16] While the identity of the novel-form as middle-class art has often been partly related to its physical existence as costly manufactured article and possession, suited to the private entertainment of the lone and leisured reader, a modified phenomenon is apparent here. When Fred Ball describes the Upton Sinclair of *The Jungle* and the Jack London of *The People of the Abyss* and *The Iron Heel* as 'the most borrowed novelists' prior to the Great War, he refers to a process of dissemination beyond the bookshop and the public library where novel-reading has become potentially more sociable, and subversive of the 'ideal' relationship of novel and individual reader in the usual formulation.[17] Personal transaction substitutes for received judgement for reasons which may not be simply, or exclusively, economic.

This context of reading – an antipole of the Edwardian bookman's world of competitive acquisition of, and solitary delight in, 'the particular copy'[18] – is one in which Tressell participated in Hastings. Collecting a library from secondhand-book shops, he lent items to workmates at a penny a week; his daughter, talking about Tressell's books and pictures, remembers that her father 'was such that if anybody wanted anything and he could possibly give it to them, he'd give it'.[19] That context of reading and dissemination entered into the shaping of *The Ragged Trousered Philanthropists*, and the novel re-entered that environment to achieve its mode of existence. It is also dramatically present within the book. Tressell's hero Frank Owen possesses 'a little library of Socialist books and pamphlets which he lent to those he hoped to influence' (394). His unconverted work-mates scorn 'fellows who had been contaminated by contact with Socialists or whose characters had been warped and degraded by the perusal of socialist literature' (424). When one expresses indignation at his treatment at work, the others 'supposed it was through readin' all those books what Owen was always lendin' 'im' (446). Lady Bell's contemporaneous enquiry into working-class reading-habits shows novels read in more than a quarter of her sample households and recognizes that books are 'handed round and read by several people'. In reading patterns often determined by 'what comes under their hand, what is suggested to them, and what they see being read by the person next door', lending takes on significance.[20] The

[15]M. Eagleton and D. Pierce, *Attitudes to Class in the English Novel from Walter Scott to David Storey* (London, Thames and Hudson, 1979), p. 79.

[16]Cit. J. B. Mitchell, *Robert Tressell and 'The Ragged Trousered Philanthropists'* (London, Lawrence and Wishart, 1969), p. 2.

[17]Ball, *Life*, p. 213.

[18]A. Waugh, *Reticence in Literature* (London, J. G. Wilson, 1915), p. 103ff.

[19]S. Douglass, ed., 'Talking to Kathleen Tressell', *Labour Monthly* L (1968), p. 263; Ball, *Life*, p. 107.

[20]Lady Bell, 'Reading Habits in Middlesborough', from *At the Works* (1907), in P. J. Keating, ed., *Into Unknown England: Selections from the Social Explorers* (Manchester,

mode of existence Tressell envisaged for his book and projected within its pages, encompasses such working-class habits and articulates them to the political activism inherent in the passing of the socialist pamphlet from hand to hand. The tradition of the novel may not supply the most telling analogy for Tressell's book so much as, for example, the penny *Pass on Pamphlets* issued from September 1908 by the Clarion Press with the instruction 'READ and PASS ON'.[21] Remembering that Tressell may have attempted pamphlets for the Hastings SDF, Nettleton's supposition that Tressell 'started writing pamphlets and at some stage . . . decided to put them together in a novel' appeals even more as a clue to the mode of his writing in *The Ragged Trousered Philanthropists* than as a literal account of its genesis.[22] There was certainly undesigned aptness in a wartime edition carrying the instruction 'For the Forces. Leave this book at any Post Office when you have read it, so that men and women in the services may enjoy it too'.[23]

Readers have tended to associate their own interaction with the text with the contexts in which they have encountered it and have been impelled to testify to such circumstances of the text's reading, outside dominant cultural channels, as epitomizing the experience of the book. The word 'cult', suggesting a self-congratulatory exclusiveness, does not capture this tradition of reading, yet *The Ragged Trousered Philanthropists* has elicited a protective pride in its readers, an awareness of guardianship and a solidarity with the text and Tressell himself. That solidarity has moved working people to establish Noonan's biography, to locate and purchase the novel-manuscript, to bring about publication of an unabridged edition, and even to brave a half-demolished church to conserve something of Tressell's decorative painting.[24] Such readers have not allowed the text to rest as the commercial novel provided for the contemplation of the lone reader. They have sidestepped the bookshop in order to share it, taken it to the building-site, the political meeting and the theatre.[25] It has been lent and given, recommended, dramatized, excerpted, learned by heart, quoted, taught, discussed, performed, watched, photographed, and, most strikingly, imitated – as Bert Hogenkamp again recalls:

> Strengthened by the result of the strike, Jackson and his comrades extended their trade union activities. At lunchhours Jackson and others led discussions on evolution and on current political topics, very much like Owen in Robert Tressell's *Ragged Trousered Philanthropists*.[26]

Manchester University Press, 1976), pp. 285–303.
[21]R. Blatchford, *Britain for the British* (London, Clarion Press, 1908), p. 175. Early titles included 'John Bull and Doctor Socialism'; 'John Bull and Doctor Free Trade'; 'John Bull and Doctor Protection'; 'Why Women Want Socialism'; 'Nationalization of Inventions'.
[22]Nettleton, 'Liverpool', p. 165.
[23]Ball, *Life*, p. 186.
[24]Op. cit., pp. 245–52. For examples of Tressell's painting see The Robert Tressell Workshop, *The Robert Tressell Papers* (Rochester, WEA, 1982), pp. 47, 72; J. Beeching, '*The Ragged Trousered Philanthropists*', *Our Time* VII (1948), p. 199.
[25]Ball, *Life*, p. 215.
[26]Hogenkamp, 'Films', pp. 262–3.

What distinguishes *The Ragged Trousered Philanthropists* from other novels of socialist propaganda is the extent to which it recognizes its own status as propaganda and offers itself for *use* as much as contemplation. It depicts suffering; it also persuades the reader to recognize the cause of that suffering. But it also promotes the activity of persuasion itself, presents it as feasible, insists upon it as an activity in which the reader can engage and in which it may itself be redeployed by that active reader. Here lies the problem of evaluating Tressell's novel for a liberal literary criticism responsive to the portrayal of dreadful working and living conditions, but which hardly knows what to do with, say, Larry Meath's disquisition on capital in *Love on the Dole*, or the last chapters of *The Jungle* in which Jurgis Rudkus discovers socialism at a political meeting. Recourse is often had to devaluing such episodes as inadequately dramatized or as failing to harmonize with modes of address established elsewhere in the writings concerned – or to according value and interest only to such non-didactic features as may be isolated.

Symptoms of this critical dilemma appear in Eagleton and Pierce's discussion.[27] Appropriately locating *The Ragged Trousered Philanthropists* within a tradition of writing concerned, in Morris's phrase, to 'make Socialists', they experience difficulty in articulating such a priority – and the role of didacticism within it – to traditional novelistic virtues. In relating Tressell's writing to both naturalism and the 'allegorical vigour' of Dickens, they are left unwilling to regard explicitly didactic modes of address as successful writing. Hence the political content is 'often obtrusive and poorly integrated'. That obtrusiveness is undeniable, although the *jouissance* of such obtrusiveness may not be a fault in writing designed to undermine repressive structures of common sense and make socialists in a non-socialist society. Moreover, obtrusiveness need not mean poor integration. Chapter 1's explicit conversation about the causes of poverty certainly constitutes political content in high relief. Here are foregrounded the principal contemporary explanations which Frank Owen must counter: idleness, drunkenness, over-population, female labour, mechanization, foreign competition, over-education, early marriage. But politics also lies in a counterpoint between the debate and the behaviour of the workmen. Over-ready to suspect the destitute apprentice Bert of appropriating their tea-money by skimping on ingredients, they fail to respond to the actuality of such exploitation in their relationship with the bosses. When the true villain emerges as the sycophantic coddie Crass, the irony is compounded. Willing to combine to place a bet (as later they buy beer and organize the 'beano'), they reject the possibility of combining to change their world. Significantly neither Frank nor Barrington join the betting syndicate. Later the workmen assert their freedom as Britons ('who never shall be slaves'), only to scatter frenziedly back to work when they anticipate the foreman's return. Such dramatic comment on the obtrusive level of the debate allows the workmen's actions to undermine their own positions.

[27]Eagleton and Pierce, *Class*, pp. 79–83.

Most distortive, however, is the tendency for aesthetic judgements to reflect doubt on a whole ethos of working-class political awareness: 'the book is full of set-pieces where the workmen conveniently fill their lunch-time breaks listening to Owen's or Barrington's lectures, complete with diagrams'. Strictures on form ('set-pieces'; 'complete with diagrams') breed scepticism about the possibility of the activity represented: lunch-times spent in political discussion apparently reflect the author's convenience rather than any imaginable workmen's. Yet one hardly needs the evidence of Hogenkamp and Nettleton to query such scepticism. It also disregards Tressell's careful dramatic handling of the lectures, both in themselves and in their contextualization through the book.

Raymond Williams produces a strikingly different valuation in remarking that Tressell

> includes – it is the most radical innovation in his work, often sitting uneasily with the other writing but there it is, and extraordinarily successful – the two interventions which do what to this day the fiction textbooks tell you you can't do, I mean the two teaching chapters 'The Oblong' and 'The Great Oration'.[28]

Slightly uneasy, even in his confidence of the writing's success, Williams actually understates the extent of the phenomenon of 'teaching': it is just as apparent in Chapter 21 ('The Great Money Trick') and in Nora's tuition of Frankie in Chapter 6. Indeed, it occurs in short episodes and conversations throughout, and in the merging apparent between the tone and concerns of Frank's lectures and the narrative voice. But in the chapters Williams adduces Tressell is arguably involved most pointedly in objectifying the process of persuasion. This technique implicates the reader in the process of persuasion as subject as well as object, by imaging such favoured characters as Frank and Barrington, with whom identification can be made, as propagandists within the fictional world. Here the activity of persuasion is firmly placed within the frame of the art-work. Frank does not lapse uncharacteristically into preaching because of his author's inability to dramatize; he is a workman whose additional dramatic identity as propagandist is essential to the reader's capacity not just to receive ideas but to construct a heroic image of the self as propagandist.

But do such emphases of interpretation square with Tressell's declarations in his preface? There he seems to aspire to familiar novelistic virtues, emphasizing the end of realistically portraying the workmen's conditions and speaking of treating socialism only 'incidentally'. But, significantly, the publication of his manuscript is only a hypothesis in the preface. The reader interpellated is a future interested publisher, one to be reassured (not wholly candidly) on the score of religion, to be primed to defend the novel with ready-made arguments about truth to life and specificity of locale, and one encouraged to find 'a readable story full of human interest

[28]R. Williams, 'The Robert Tressell Memorial Lecture, 1982', *HWJ* 16 (1983), p. 78.

and based on the happenings of everyday life' (12). Such comments have their relevance, but Tressell thereby engineers generic expectations likely to play on an awareness of the East End fiction of Gissing, Morrison or Besant, of the descents into the abyss of Blatchford, Wyckoff and London, and even of the popular sketches of working-class life by William Pett Ridge, a writer appearing in such high-circulation magazines as the *Strand* and the *English Illustrated*.[29] Tressell tactically anticipates the grounds on which a publisher might be tempted to back the book – as Grant Richards eventually was when he placed greater weight on the 'extraordinarily real' in the book than on its being 'damnably subversive'.[30] In the novel, however, the controlling strategy is to present the case for socialism and the problem of its dissemination. Even where Tressell seems most the novelist committed to an impression of life and character, his art is infused with argument. Chapter 3, for example, first impresses as a slice of life in which a couple discuss their finances in a universally recognizable way, seeking the reader's sympathy for the poor in a manner familiar from nineteenth-century fiction. Emotions are stirred, most movingly when the couple tacitly agree to deceive themselves about the reasons for their baby's sickness, most bitterly when their finances are ironically demolished by the demand for the Poor Rate. But the scene is also overlaid upon a clinically particular set of figures about basic living standards and weekly income and expenditure. The trajectory of the scene lies in Easton's gradual compilation of these figures. The reader encounters not Micawber's symbolic equations or Jo's dissolving sovereign, but an imagination retaining hold on shillings and pence and an intimate appreciation of domestic contingencies. Beneath Easton's list there ghosts a tradition of table-making – part social-scientific, part rhetorical – present in works by William Booth, Seebohm Rowntree and W.B.N., and leading on to deployment by Margaret Pember Reeves, Orwell and Wal Hannington.[31] The statistics of the social survey of the poor and the *exempla* of the political propagandist underpin the scene, uncompromising figures which require intellectual as well as emotional response. This is not merely the animation of statistics, or the demonstration of Easton's plight as representative. The organicism of Tressell's politically committed observation presents a human suffering inextricable from the particularities of the economic system producing it. To evade the book's political imperative is thus to deal only with a shadow of the writing, to risk deceiving oneself with the 1957 *TLS* reviewer that the book survives as 'a story', while the

[29]E.g., G. Gissing, *The Nether World* (1889); A. Morrison, *A Child of the Jago* (1896); W. Besant, *All Sorts and Conditions of Men* (1882); R. Blatchford, *Dismal England* (1899); W. Wyckoff, *The Workers – The West* (1899); J. London, *The People of the Abyss* (1903); W. Pett Ridge, *Up Side-Streets* (1903). See also P. J. Keating, *The Working Classes in Victorian Fiction* (London, Routledge and Kegan Paul, 1971).
[30]Cit. Ball, *Life*, p. 167.
[31]W. Booth, *In Darkest England and the Way Out* (1890); B. S. Rowntree, *Poverty: A Study of Town Life* (1901); W. B. N., *Penal Servitude* (1903); M. Pember Reeves, *Round About a Pound a Week* (1913); G. Orwell, *The Road to Wigan Pier* (1937); W. Hannington, *The Problem of the Distressed Areas* (1937).

political content is merely 'half-baked', threatening to 'swamp' the characters.[32]

The Ragged Trousered Philanthropists deployed the book as weapon in the battle for socialists against existing Tory, Liberal, Christian, Temperance and Philanthropic propaganda. Ball understands Tressell's lending of books to his workmates as an effort to counter 'pernicious teaching' and the influence of the yellow press and the religious tract.[33] Tressell wrote his novel as the ideal book to lend in that battle.

Stephen Yeo describes the special role of books in socialist conversion in the 1890s. Indeed, in depicting their mode of existence in the Labour Church, and in tracing the 'escape into collective use' of such writings, Yeo provides a model analogous to that underlying the urge towards the multiform dissemination of *The Ragged Trousered Philanthropists* sketched above:

> Works like *Towards Democracy*, *Merrie England*, or *News from Nowhere* were gulped thirstily into the consciousness of groups of workers, and were used as integral parts of socialist life. There would be silence, demand for more, and then 'reading on their own account by the listeners'. Similarly, collections of labour hymns, songs and 'Chants for Socialists' showed that poems escaped from books, or the newspapers which printed them, such as *The Workman's Times* or *Clarion*, into collective use.[34]

Tressell's novel continues the function within socialist life and proselytism of such writings as Carpenter's, Blatchford's and Morris's. Moreover, the book functions to assist the 'escape into collective use' of the ideas and arguments of such texts. David Smith has indicated Tressell's use of earlier socialist writings, involving borrowing from Bellamy, Blatchford, Wells and Morris as well as Marx.[35] Here an analogy is worth making with Blatchford's *Merrie England* and *Britain for the British*, non-fictional socialist polemics in which Blatchford quotes other writers prolifically and supplies bibliographies of items he now wishes 'John Smith' to read. Providing nutshell arguments as 'trump cards' and directing reading are primary means in Blatchford's enlisting his reader under socialism. Tressell integrates such reading into the arguments of Frank, Barrington and Nora. Plagiarism – or poverty of imagination – is not an issue: working-class intellectuals and Fabians would know such arguments and would hardly credit Tressell with their origination, or theft. Moreover, the title-page dissolves the individual identity of Robert Noonan as acclaim-seeking author into the representative identity of 'Robert Tressell' – Trestle the

[32]Cit. Ball, *Life*, p. 203.
[33]Op. cit., p. 107.
[34]S. Yeo, 'A New Life: The Religion of Socialism in Britain, 1883–1896', *HWJ* 4 (1977), p. 29.
[35]D. Smith, *Socialist Propaganda in the Twentieth-Century British Novel* (London, Macmillan, 1978), p. 28.

workman, kin to Hodge the labourer. The novel serves the collective thought, experience and ends of socialism rather than the personality and kudos of a private author. This is apparent when young Frankie explains socialism to a friendly tradesman and incidentally sketches precisely the context in which *The Ragged Trousered Philanthropists* is designed to operate:

> 'I promised to lend him some literature. You won't mind, will you Dad?'
> 'Of course not; when we get home we'll have a look through what we've got and you can take him some of them.'
> 'I know!' cried Frankie eagerly. 'The two very best of all. *Happy Britain* and *England for the English.*'
> He knew that these were 'two of the best' because he had often heard his father and mother say so, and he had noticed that whenever a Socialist friend came to visit them, he was also of the same opinion.   (244)

Tressell's book is a self-contained kit for the dissemination of ideas, the 'Great Money Trick' episode, aided by Thomas's projection of it, having been the most frequently used component – a mechanism facilitating the escape into collective use of the theory of surplus value. Indeed, when Greenwood had Larry Meath deliver a version of Tressell's Great Money Trick he fulfilled a purpose of Tressell's. The nutshell lesson has been communicated to a reader (Greenwood), and disseminated further (through *Love on the Dole*) with encouragement of the new audience to continue dissemination (through a parallel use of the objectified lecture).[36] Blatchford spells out what Tressell implicitly seeks to achieve:

> Meanwhile, I ask you, as a reader of this book, not to sit down in despair with the feeling that the workers will not move, but try to move them. Be you *one*, John Smith. Be you the first. Then you shall surely win a few, and so are multitudes composed.
>   . . . if you approve of this little book I shall be glad if you will recommend it to your friends.[37]

That end was also intuited by Thomas. In his adaptation's final scene, Joe Philpot (apparently converted by Frank) puts to the audience a motion calling for membership of unions and the advent of socialism. The curtain descends, according to the 1936 stage-directions, 'on a great cry of "AYE" from the audience'.[38] This closure unites the dramatic trajectory with the unfolding extension of the process of persuasion. At the end of the unabridged novel the reader knows Frank's health is failing, but also that Barrington will return reinforced to Mugsborough. Novel-readers, of course, cannot give a communal shout of 'AYE', but identifying with

[36]W. Greenwood, *Love on the Dole* (London, Jonathan Cape, 1933), pp. 239–45.
[37]Blatchford, *Britain*, p. 172.
[38]Thomas, *Philanthropists*, p. 89.

Barrington as well as Frank they can make the sociable gesture of recommending the book and passing it on.

The nickname 'The Painter's Bible' highlights an aspect of that creation of identification. A 'bible' or 'book of words' is a familiar manual of techniques and instruction, an authoritative source of guidance in a workman's particular trade. Irony certainly plays about the application of the term to Tressell's book, but there is also an unironic link. Frank is highly skilled. Both he and Tressell deplore the corruption of valued professional skills. Detecting this concern, the reader is enabled to construct Frank as the ideal workman of the bibles. Tressell appropriates the authority of a literary figure and genre familiar to skilled working-class readers and articulates that authority to Frank's other role as socialist propagandist. Ellis Davidson's bible, for example, implies an ideal workman closely resembling Frank, a man working in country towns rather than London, who is at once skilled as 'house painter, grainer, letter painter and gilder'.[39] Frank's creation of the Moorish room depends on his conversancy with the techniques and spirit of such a manual as Davidson's, which, combining Morris, Ruskin and Owen Jones with a dash of Smiles, freely refers to medieval manuscript illumination, printing history and the techniques of Cimabue, Fra Angelico and Giotto. Frank has been craftsman-trained in contrast to both Crass, who impresses bosses with a smattering of terminology about 'tones', 'shades' and 'harmony' (50), and Sawkins, a labourer who 'having armed himself with a putty knife and put on a white jacket, regarded himself as a fully qualified painter' (15). Davidson characteristically urges employers and unions to improve technical education and specifically to assemble model examples of graining and marbling. In the novel Frank takes on this role, compensating for the bosses' neglect. While rejecting technical education as the answer to poverty, Frank uses spare time to prepare patterns of graining for Bert White, instructs him in lettering and gives him an old set of graining combs – as well as teaching him at work. Thus Frank harmonizes with the spirit of the bibles. The analogue of the bible is also maintained through Tressell's style, which often savours more of instruction than description:

> To fix such a paper as this properly the walls should first be done with a plain lining paper of the same colour as the ground of the wallpaper itself, because unless the paperhanger 'lapps' the joints – which should not be done – they are apt to open a little as the paper dries and to show the white wall underneath.   (433)

Utilizing graphics to present Rushton's card and time-sheet and the poster for Barrington's oration also recalls the familiar model signs and lettering displays of the bibles. In such a text Frank is constructable not as the work-shy firebrand of popular prejudice, but as ideal workman who is

---

[39]E. A. Davidson, *A Practical Manual of House-Painting, Graining, Marbling and Sign-Writing* (10th edn, London, Crosby Lockwood, 1911), p. 22.

1. Front cover of *The British Workman* LVIII (1913).

Interesting the Painters.

2. 'Clean Literature: How it is circulated. The Christian Colportage Association 1874–1912', from *The British Workman* LVIII (1913), pp. 22–3.

Children frequently Influence Sales.

3. 'Clean Literature . . .'

THE MOCKERY OF FREE SPEECH.

4. Illustration to H. Murray, 'The Mockery of Free Speech. An Appeal to British Workmen', *The British Workman* LVII (1912), p. 25.

compatibly a socialist propagandist. The reader is thus firmly positioned to view the propaganda battle Tressell reveals within his society.

Invisible to its inhabitants, ideology-forming apparatuses infest Mugsborough. Sweater and Grinder control the newspapers: the *Daily Obscurer*, with Captain Kiddem's sporting columns and Mrs Prosser's 'Original Parables'; the *Weekly Ananias* and the *Daily Chloroform* – mystification, hypocrisy and anaesthesia. The popular press, exemplified by Bert's *Chronicles of Crime*, 'penny instalments of the adventures of Claude Duval' and *Orange Blossoms*, hypnotizes pedestrians into colliding (literally and symbolically) with the workmen's ladders (430). Significantly, Bert eventually appropriates images for his propagandist 'Pandorama' from 'pictures cut out of weekly illustrated papers and pasted together' (324).

Socially conformist religious propaganda is evident in the Sunday magazines 'dispensing advice on "Christian Duty" ', the Moody and Sankey hymns on the workmen's lips, and the books that enter working-class homes even when no others do – the Bible and Sunday school prizes. The Eastons' 'brightly bound books' (51) are clearly such prizes, intimated by the hanging photograph of Sunday school girls (doubtless including Ruth). Probably publications of the Religious Tract Society, the National Temperance League, or an improving publisher such as S. W. Partridge with their periodicals the *Children's Friend* and the *British Workman* (motto: *'laborare est orare'*), they occupy one table while Mrs Starvem's Bible oppresses another. Propaganda-machines, Sunday schools reward ideology uncritically absorbed with even more propaganda:

> 'I'm going to 'ave a prize next Sunday at our Sunday School,' said Elsie, as they were leaving.
> 'What are you going to get it for?' asked Nora.
> ''Cause I learned my text properly. I had to learn the whole of the first chapter of Matthew by heart and I never made one single mistake! So teacher said she'd give me a nice book next Sunday.'
> 'I 'ad one too, the other week, about six months ago, didn't I, Elsie?' said Charley.   (144)

Chillingly, the children leave Frankie's party for the Band of Hope Tea and Prize Distribution. Adults lured into lectures on 'their duty to their betters' elicit Tressell's contempt:

> Most of them belonged to these P.S.A.s for the sake of the loaves and fishes. Every now and then they were awarded prizes – *Self-help* by Smiles, and other books suitable for perusal by persons suffering from almost complete obliteration of the mental faculties.   (492)

No oppositional popular culture challenges the ideological power of the established hegemony. Acknowledging that 'nearly everyone spends money on some hobby', Tressell shows little beyond Tom Linden's magical fretwork clock-case (linked by non-Christian imagery of domes and pinnacles to Frank's decorative work and the final vision of the Co-operative Commonwealth). But Tom has died in the Boer War, and Sweater, through Didlum, eventually appropriates the clock-case. Jack Mitchell argues, unsatisfactorily, for pub-life as a centre of resilience, but Tressell finds only opiates: 'there was a penny-in-the-slot piano at the Blue Lion and as that was the last house of the road they made a rather long stop there, playing hooks and rings, shove-ha'penny, drinking, dancing and finally quarrelling' (488).[40] Drink depressingly dominates working-class entertainment and Tressell pointedly casts Frank as teetotaller. Football promises no more than racing, theatres and music halls no more than menageries and circuses.

Pessimism about the dependence of working-class culture forces Tressell towards direct political education rather than struggle through cultural forms – where the battle is already lost.[41] Counter-cultural potential exists in Bert's Pandorama, but Tressell rather presents it as one means of direct education among many: the lecture to workmates, role-playing, child-rearing, book-lending, the individual's purchase and distribution of pamphlets, confronting opponents' propaganda, flags, standards, marches, even propaganda from bicycles and travelling vans. Opportunities exist for counter-propaganda inside and outside the novel where convictions may become actions and the arguments and *exempla* of the novel itself be redeployed.

The propagandist's task is not presented as easy: Frank is often nervous and depressed, and his auditors' difficulties in thinking and reading critically are never understated. Alternately suspicious of books and credulous towards anything printed, they challenge courage and stamina. But other interests had the task in hand. The *British Workman*, for example, had long groomed a docile respectability. Keen to celebrate the dissemination of 'pure' literature among such as Tressell's painters, it continued projecting images of the ideal workman and the abomination of the atheistic demagogue. History might have been kinder had it preserved the banner Tressell designed for the SDF rather than his church panel with the text 'Thy Word is a Lamp unto my Feet and a Light unto my Path'.[42]

[40]Mitchell, *Tressell*, pp. 172–3
[41]See H. Cunningham, *Leisure in the Industrial Revolution* (London, Croom Helm, 1980).
[42]Workshop, *Papers*, p. 33.

Note

This essay attempts to juxtapose and connect different modes of novel-writing centred on the mining industry or the mining community: from the bourgeois-socialist novelist Emile Zola's *Germinal* (1885) and the exiled working-class novelist D.H. Lawrence's *Sons and Lovers* (1913) and *Lady Chatterley's Lover* (1928), to those novelists of the 1930s who represent proletarian fiction proper, adult workers writing from within the class. Walter Brierley's *Means-Test Man* (1935), and Lewis Jones's *Cwmardy* (1937) and *We Live* (1939) appear as examples of fiction by miners. *A Kestrel for a Knave* (1969) and *The Price of Coal* (1982) exemplify the work of a contemporary writer, Barry Hines, who worked in the mining industry before becoming a teacher. The essay has adhered throughout to accessible texts: though a complete picture of the genre would necessarily have to incorporate novels unobtainable except from specialist libraries. Of particular interest among these are W.E. Tirebuck's *Miss Grace of All Souls* (London, Heinemann, 1895); James C. Welsh's *The Underworld* (London, Herbert Jenkins, 1920); Harold Heslop's *Last Cage Down* (London, Wishart Books, 1935); and Len Doherty's *A Miner's Sons* (London, Lawrence and Wishart, 1955), and *The Man Beneath* (London, Lawrence & Wishart, 1957). Lawrence and Wishart plan to reissue some 1930s proletarian novels, possibly including some mining fiction.

I would like to thank Dr Hywel Francis of the South Wales Miners' Library for providing me with material for this study.

2

Miners and the Novel: From Bourgeois to Proletarian Fiction

Graham Holderness

There seems, at last, to be some point in talking about the existence of a British working-class novel: the long task of recovering, theoretically and practically, this rich seam of oppositional culture is seriously under way. In fact the theoretical work has outstripped the pace of practical restoration, and thereby inevitably embraced damaging constraints: until the texts of working-class novels from the nineteenth and early twentieth centuries are reprinted and educationally mobilized on a much larger scale, there can be no effective general recovery to shift radically the political balance of the literary tradition. On the other hand, some of the texts have reappeared as a direct consequence of critical attention from writers dependent for their sources on specialist libraries. This poverty of material in circulation has entailed an inevitable but dangerous concentration on a handful of texts which already seem doomed to canonization as the great tradition of proletarian fiction: Robert Tressell's *The Ragged-Trousered Philanthropists* (1914): Lewis Jones's *Cwmardy* and *We Live* (1937, 1939); Lewis Grassic Gibbon's *A Scots Quair* (1932–4). Anyone writing on this subject will experience difficulty in balancing the contradictory pressures and constraints: the need to discuss those texts your readers can share with you; and the need to reject any such privileging of individual masterpieces as the authentic voice of a whole class and culture.

We ought therefore to be considering alternative theoretical perspectives, before the individual texts we recover are smoothly incorporated as the dark underside of a global system: the house of literature has many mansions, and the proprietors are continually building extensions. Necessary theoretical distinctions have been attempted but not yet carried through: between working-class and proletarian literature;[1] between class-conscious and politically committed socialist literature;[2] between the author who travels beyond the working class and the author who writes from within it;[3] between the fiction of a region (geographical and social)

---

[1] Roy Johnson, 'The Proletarian Novel', *Literature and History* 2 (1975).
[2] H. Gustav Klaus, 'Introduction' to his own edited anthology *The Socialist Novel in Britain* (Brighton, Harvester Press, 1982).
[3] Raymond Williams, 'Working-Class, Proletarian, Socialist: Problems in some Welsh

and the fiction of a nation, the novel of a class and a community, and the novel of an entire social system.[4] I propose to experiment in this essay with another, more historical and aesthetic than political, category: fiction based on and growing out of a particular industrial formation and the specific community associated with that formation. To isolate 'mining novels' from other kinds of working-class fiction may seem unnecessary or even perverse, given the historical participation of the miners in the broader labour movement, and the kind of trade-union unity forged between them and other sections of the organized working class. But to ground fiction in the type of labour, social community and political organization characteristic of a particular industry offers several opportunities: to historicize our conceptions of literary production and consumption; to theorize more precisely the distinction between the bourgeois and the working-class novel; and to delineate the specific aesthetic problems encountered by a discourse originating in and committed to such an industry, such a class and community, such forms of economic production, social organization and political struggle.

I

Raymond Williams has observed that despite its centrality as a basic industry (and, we might add, its early intensive development of capitalist social relations and its vitality as a source of working-class militancy), the coalmining industry received little more than glancing recognition in the nineteenth-century bourgeois industrial novel.[5] That significant absence was not mere absent-mindedness or anachronism, but a systematic writing of a society's industrial base out of its dominant literary form. Where the bourgeois novel does glimpse the landscapes of the coalmining industry, its specific conditions of labour, and the character of its workers, they appear as distinctively alien to the normative reality constituted by the form:

> They come forth; the mine delivers its gang and the pit its bondsmen; the forge is silent and the engine is still. The plain is covered with the swarming multitude: bands of stalwart men, broad-chested and muscular, wet with toil, and black as the children of the tropics . . . can we wonder at the hideous coarseness of their language, when we remember the savage rudeness of their lives?[6]

> As the day wore on, the scene would change: the land would begin to be blackened with coal-pits, the rattle of handlooms to be heard in hamlets and villages. Here were powerful men walking queerly with knees bent

Novels', in Klaus, *The Socialist Novel*.
[4]Raymond Williams, 'Region and Class in the Novel', in Douglas Jefferson and Graham Martin, eds., *The Uses of Fiction: Essays on the Modern Novel in Honour of Arnold Kettle* (Milton Keynes, Open University Press, 1982).
[5]Williams, 'Working-Class, Proletarian, Socialist', p. 113.
[6]Benjamin Disraeli, *Sybil, or the Two Nations* (1845).

outward from squatting in the mine, going home to throw themselves down in their blackened flannel and sleep through the daylight. . . .[7]

In Disraeli's biblical cadences an acknowledgement of the primitive physical power visible in the labouring mass co-exists with an emphasis on blackness and 'savagery' as the self-evident signs of foreign-ness, a fascinating and frightening otherness. The reader is required to share ('can we wonder?') the narrator's detached combination of moral disapprobation and externalized solicitude. George Eliot's narrator is equally distanced from the 'scene' she depicts, in an apparently objective documentary delineation of social conditions: and again we find the frightened respect for a 'power' in the miners, mingled with a sense of distorted reality, men 'walking queerly' to their strange and unnatural daylight sleep. Perhaps the final culmination of this external representation appears in science-fiction: in the dystopian world of H.G. Wells's *The Time Machine* (1895), where a separate human species has colonized the depths of the earth, to live in a system of underground shafts and tunnels ventilated by electric power. The weird inhumanity and alien power of the Morlocks represent this bourgeois conception of the miners, evolved to an ultimate extremity of estrangement and terror.

II

The mining novel proper could be said to begin with a remarkable bourgeois-socialist text, Emile Zola's *Germinal* (1885). In its establishing of the mining community as the social world of the novel, its use of economic conditions and political struggles as plot and action, and its postulation of an active proletarian community as collective 'hero', it founded a characteristic form followed by Lewis Jones, Harold Heslop, Len Doherty and others. This novel's combination of meticulously-researched documentary realism, and its continuation of the device of 'estrangement' which was bourgeois fiction's characteristic vision of the mining world, established parameters which remain persistently useful for the analysis of this type of writing. Zola saw his fiction as scientific realism, and hoped to establish in *Germinal* the truth of a broad social situation by appealing to 'facts, not emotional pleas'. Yet the emotional intensity of Zola's representation constantly disturbs the balanced externality of documentary statement, and involves the reader in a peculiar dialectic of empathy and alienation: drawing the engaged consciousness towards an imaginative solidarity with the exploited working class and a liberating fantasy of socialist revolution; and simultaneously thrusting it away from the agents of that revolution as the spectres of a terrifying vengeance:

Men were springing up, a black avenging host was slowly germinating in

7George Eliot, *Felix Holt the Radical* (1866).

the furrows, thrusting upwards for the harvests of future ages. And very soon their germination would crack the earth asunder.[8]

John Berger has demonstrated that the root of these contradictions was the 'gap' which always exists between a bourgeois writer and his proletarian subjects: a gap of experience which renders the worker's life 'mysterious' to an outsider's vision.

> For Zola, because of the extremity of the poverty and injustice he was witnessing, this gap, this mysterious aspect of a miner's life, was much more blatant . . . his researches, his investigations, his visits, brought him to the edge of an unbridgeable abyss: an abyss between the condition of his own life as a writer and the condition of those whose lives he was writing about. . . . And at the level of his imagination, he recognized this. Despite all his claims to be scientific, despite all his research, *Germinal* is essentially a book about a dream. . . . And this dream, which was often a nightmare, was born out of what Zola could not know about his subject-matter. And into that space, into that gap, which disturbed him profoundly, he projected his conscious and unconscious fears and hopes. . . .[9]

On the basis of this contradictory *rapprochement* of ideologies and aesthetic devices – liberal-reformism allied with utopian socialism, documentary naturalism clashing with symbolist and surrealist techniques – Zola was able to perceive the mining industry both as a solid reality, stubbornly resistant to change, and as a kind of fiction, dream, or nightmare.[10]

Throughout *Germinal* the mine is seen with this double focus: as a material fact, part of a particular economic system; and as a mythological monster, a diabolical and bestial creature which devours men and women, feeding on their labour and destroying their lives.[11] In the strike the organized workers of the coalfield attempt to confront the system as a material fact: they succeed only in inflicting some marginal damage, and economic power, governed by remote and alien forces and conditions, ultimately eludes them. The mine as a mythological monster is however confronted and destroyed in its lair by an individual dragonslayer, in the form of the anarchist Souvarine – whose cold, impersonal and inhuman will makes him the counterpart, as well as the opposite, of the alien beast he annihilates.

This then was the legacy inherited by the working-class mining novelist from the bourgeois novel. Because of the 'gap' of class and experience separating him from the labouring people, the sensitive and radical bour-

---

[8]Emile Zola, *Germinal* (1885; trans. Leonard Tancock, London, Penguin, 1954), p. 499.
[9]John Berger, *Germinal: a Discussion* (Open University/B.B.C.–television programme, 1972).
[10]See Zola, p. 20.
[11]See op. cit., p. 21.

geois writer perceived the industry and its people as strange, alien, 'other'; however strongly his imagination may have been attracted by that strangeness, or his political sympathies stimulated by the vision of an oppressed but vigorous and socialized working class, his writing must needs disclose that distance, and represent the industrial system as an alien force confronting an impotent people; a force which could be destroyed, but never economically transformed, politically controlled and socially organized. It would appear from this that the first task confronting a working-class novelist (defined here, for the moment, as a writer born into the working class, whether or not he remained within it), whose experience has closed the gap between writer and working class, would be to attempt a demystification of that mythological vision, a recovery and repossession of those estranged and alienated powers. It would seem to be necessary, in order to transform the bourgeois novel's representation of mining life to present the miners and their families naturalistically, as human beings, capable both of patient everyday endurance and of disciplined collective struggle; to present the social life of the mining village as a knowable community, a model both of the conflict-ridden industrial system and of a potential future society of equality and co-operation; and to present the industry itself as a material object capable of being politically and economically transformed into a new democratic system of social organization. Which brings us, first, to D.H. Lawrence.

III

In summer, the pits are often slack. Often on bright sunny mornings, the men are seen trooping home again at ten, eleven or twelve o'clock. No empty trucks stand at the pit-mouth. The women on the hillside look across as they shake the hearthrug against the fence, and count the waggons the engine is taking along the line up the valley. And the children, as they come from school at dinner-time, looking down the fields and seeing the wheels on the headstocks standing, say:

'Minton's knocked off. My dad'll be at home'. And there is a sort of shadow over all, women and children and men, because money will be short at the end of the week.[12]

Incarnate ugliness, and yet alive! What would become of them all? Perhaps with the passing of the coal they would disappear again, off the face of the earth. They had appeared out of nowhere in their thousands, when the coal had called for them. Perhaps they were only weird fauna of the coal-seams. Creatures of another reality, they were elementals, serving the elements of coal, as the metal-workers were elementals, serving the element of iron. Men not men, but anima of coal and iron and clay.[13]

[12]D.H. Lawrence, *Sons and Lovers* (1913; London, Penguin, 1948), p. 27.
[13]D.H. Lawrence, *Lady Chatterley's Lover* (1928; London, Penguin, 1973), p. 166.

The first passage enacts a realist language of community which is more than documentary naturalism. The technique of transparent narration, using direct statement, in the present tense, from the viewpoint of a participant in the collective experience, quietly reveals an implicit familiarity, not only with the significant details of the social landscape, but with their emotional significance, with the community's whole 'structure of feeling'. The narration is undeflected by any sense of distance, free from any deviation into the mysterious and inexplicable; and there are no embarrassed contortions of explanation addressed to the reader. The writer simply demonstrates the social and human structure of this working-class community: work and the witholding of work; the calculating anxiety of women and the naïve curiosity of children; the shadow of economic deprivation. The working-class writer, at least on this level of normative realism, has arrived.

And yet the destination of Lawrence's representation of mining life was a strangeness beyond Zola's most extravagant fantasies. *Lady Chatterley's Lover* records a vision of industrial labour as the uttermost alienation, the miners so subdued to what they work in that they have become 'elementals', inhuman creatures of the coal-seams. An extreme distantiation of perspective extrapolates the mining industry as an abstract process of mechanical production in which human workers are little more than fungi or bacteria: 'weird fauna of the coal-seams'; 'the anima of mineral disintegration'.

An easy theoretical formulation presents itself, necessarily for questioning: that Lawrence's tragic personal history of ejection from the working class restored the 'gap' between writer and community in an even more extreme form; so that the trajectory of his writing runs from an empathetic engagement with the community to a radical alienation from it. Biographically this is obviously the case: but the argument offers no adequate evaluation of these different modes of discourse and their ideological capacities. The naturalism of *Sons and Lovers* is also a *naturalization* of a community replete with contradictions, but impervious to change: and moreover the novel's realism is constantly being pushed towards and beyond the limits of that working-class community, passing into an estranging realization of whatever lies beyond its bounds (consider for example Mrs Morel's encounter with the 'mysterious out-of-doors' after a battle with her husband).[14] The reasons for that stylistic conjuncture I have elaborated elsewhere:[15] a class-conscious ideology of community and an individualist ideology of social mobility are related, to reveal, admittedly, little faith in the former, but to disclose the utter hopelessness of the latter as a means to human fulfilment and social progress. The techniques of 'estrangement' are as vital as those of naturalism to the achievement of this 'tragic realism'.[16] Furthermore, the alienated vision of the mining community in *The Rainbow*, *Women in Love*, *Lady Chatterley's Lover*, has its own

[14]Lawrence, *Sons and Lovers*, pp. 34–6.
[15]In Graham Holderness, *D.H. Lawrence: History, Ideology and Fiction* (Dublin, Gill and Macmillan, 1982), pp. 146–7.
[16]Op. cit., p. 19.

validity and value: by refusing to grant the industry the status of the natural, this fantastic discourse fundamentally questions its 'reality'. The language of the passage quoted shows men utterly subjected to an alienating system, therefore powerless to change it. But to realize that system as a kind of nightmare is certainly to acknowledge its undeniable power, *but also to insist* on its real status as an illusion, the bad dream of a society which may yet awaken to an alternative reality. What we can learn from Lawrence's writing, as from Zola's, is the indispensable function of non-naturalistic discourses in any fiction aspiring to express the full complexity of an industrial working-class community, past and future, oppression and liberation; the enduring nightmare that is, and the dream of justice yet to come.[17]

IV

Walter Brierley's *Means-Test Man* (1935), written by a Derbyshire miner, dates from the decade when economic depression, mass unemployment and the sharpening of political contradictions in Britain and in Europe pushed working-class literature into relative prominence. And Brierley's novel has generally been taken as an example of that 'naturalizing' programme outlined earlier, which seemed the most obvious function of proletarian fiction: a member of the working class writing about the specifically working-class experience of unemployment, in a technique of documentary realism; the objective being to display the facts, to tell the truth, from the insider's point-of-view. Roy Johnson criticized the novel for its 'naïve attempt at realism': 'the flat, undramatized method of presentation works against any value it might have aesthetically'.[18] Other critics, while rejecting Johnson's argument, have nevertheless accepted that Brierley's method is that of naturalism[19] or realism.[20]

Brierley's method is certainly naturalistic in the most obvious senses: it is wholly empirical, recording social facts and psychological impressions in the most literal way, scrupulously avoiding theoretical analysis or generalized reflection. Yet certain aspects of *Means-Test Man* reveal it to be a strange kind of naturalism. Jane Cook reflects on an unobtainable dress glimpsed in a shop-window:

> She turned from the window and continued towards the market; the dress did not please any longer, it had lost its definiteness and particularity, being merged into that world out of her reach. Not that she and her family were outside the world; that was where the bitterness came

[17]See Tony Bennett, *Formalism and Marxism* (London, Methuen, 1979), pp. 24–5.
[18]Roy Johnson, 'Walter Brierley: Proletarian Writing', *Red Letters* 2 (1976), p. 5.
[19]Carol Snee, 'Walter Brierley: A Test Case', *Red Letters* 3 (1976), p. 11; also 'Working-Class Literature or Proletarian Writing?', in Jon Clark *et al.*, eds., *Culture and Crisis in Britain in the 30s* (London, Lawrence and Wishart, 1979).
[20]Ramón López Ortega, 'The Language of the Working-Class Novel of the 1930s', in Klaus, *The Socialist Novel*, p. 129.

in; they were penned in a small space in the world like a lot of cattle and were provided with what was thought enough for them. Thousands of harassed men, women and children were penned with them, beings with no independence, no freedom, underfed, underclothed, not trusted. Yet from behind their barrier they could look out into the real world and see folk less intelligent, less sensitive, less capable, moving about with even minds and certain feet, taking and giving, choosing and discarding, who would think the world gone mad if a man were to come and sit at their table and demand to know every secret of their domestic life.[21]

The 'real world' is explicitly differentiated from the experience of the unemployed: they occupy a peripheral dimension of extreme deprivation, watching the world of 'normality' from behind a barrier of separation. Their condition is not simply one of poverty, but one of extreme alienation: their experience, if released into the 'even' certainty of the 'real world', would drive that world to madness. Jack Cook experiences a similar emotion as he looks at the pit in which he formerly worked: 'He had worked there ten years, the place was part of him, he was part of the place. . . . It rejected him. Such was infinitely worse than love-rejection, this was being-rejection' (87). Unemployment is the 'complete suspension of normal life', a condition of comprehensive rejection and negation. Just as our social language can express the absence of labour only by negating a positive term – *unemployment*, out of *work* – so a novel about unemployment by a *working* man (one whose defining characteristic is therefore denied by his actual experience) cannot express reality as other than a condition of alienation. The novel's preoccupation with this dichotomy is so consistent as to make that normative 'real world' almost an absent subject; with the result that the world of 'normal' labour and community appears as an ideology rather than a reality, its validity denied by the very existence on its margins of that world of the rejected and dispossessed. Jack Cook is shown to occupy a position of social and psychological 'double-bind': between his faith in the 'real world' and his existence in the actual. Since, as Carol Snee points out,[22] the dominant values of bourgeois society insist on the moral necessity of labour and on the sanctity of family and home, Jack Cook is ideologically coerced towards work, and simultaneously prevented from working; ethically committed to the autonomy of the family, actually subjected to the violating intrusion of the Means-Test inspector. The psychological consequences are vividly described:

His whole being was finely poised, the last three years' experiences had been one persistent refinement until now the very essence of him was bared, feeling pain at the mildest breath of disturbing. The mere notion that his child was suffering rushed him into a nervous sickness,

[21]Walter Brierley, *Means-Test Man* (1935); ed. Andy Croft (Nottingham, Spokesman, 1983), p. 129.
[22]Snee, 'Walter Brierley', p. 12.

holding him from action . . . If his child should be ill: the
doctor – special things, perhaps, food, medicines. Scraping along on
twenty-five shillings would be completely disorganized. His wife would
be more irritable. . . . Three minutes gone. Must be living on the edge
of suicide when little things can make you feel like this.   (15–16)

The fact that the social and psychological condition of the characters is
defined as one of extreme alienation radically alters the signifying poten-
tialities of the apparently naturalistic style. The reference to 'three minutes
gone' concerns the boiling of an egg: an operation which, like the mere
suggestion of family illness (the child is not ill), can provoke extraordinary
emotional tumults, can shatter a precarious though hard-won equilib-
rium. Each 'little thing', each minute detail of empirical observation, contains a strange otherworld of dark anxiety and existential terror; and the
naturalistic surface is constantly fracturing to disclose these underground
fears. The 'remorseless detail' with which Brierley stipulates the minutiae
of existence is not at all a sociologist's fidelity to detail (which could be
accomplished just as thoroughly by an Orwell), but an investing of details
with particular meaning: a life in which the obsessive preoccupation with
petty banalities signifies an anxious trusting in a reality which is constantly
being fissured by powers apparently beyond, but actually contained
within, its visible form.

V

Lewis Jones's *Cwmardy* (1937) and *We Live* (1939) cut a new seam of mining literature, and indeed of proletarian fiction in general. Like Brierley,
Jones wrote as an adult worker from within the class; but his representa-
tions of work and community engage with a fully developed socialist
consciousness to alter radically the nature of the novel form. Economic
conditions and political events cease to exist only as a remote, unintelligi-
ble background or even as determinant though distant tangible pressures:
they become subjects, as the class which lives through and creates them
becomes a collective 'hero': 'It is the community, and more crucially the
class which becomes the central character'.[23] As Snee acknowledges, the
novels do not entirely dispense with traditional fictional conventions, but
largely preserve naturalistic form. One traditional structural pattern is
maintained in a persistent focus on the working-class family – 'the most
accessible fictional centre, grounded in the reality of this kind of class community';[24] and the legacy of the *bildungsroman* is visible in the tracing of
Communist militant Len Roberts' career from childhood to death in
Spain. It is when Jones attempts to integrate individual emotions into the
experience of mass political action that his writing presses painfully against
the boundaries of the novel form:

[23]Op. cit., p. 187.
[24]Williams, 'Working-Class, Proletarian, Socialist', p. 116.

Again the stormy cheers moulded themselves into music that helped to marshal the ranks for the delayed march:

> 'Then raise the scarlet standard high,
> within its shade we'll live or die'.

The rhythm timed the marching feet, whose heavy 'tramp-tramp' maintained a sonorous monotone to the song. Len kept close to Mary all the way, pressing her closely to his side in the crush.

'This is life', she whispered, stretching herself to bring her lips near his ear.

'Yes', Len replied, 'because it shows the way to revolution and freedom'.

Her hand sought his, and they both joined in the singing as their feet took them on.[25]

It is a bold experiment: the language of personal tenderness is yoked with the language of military discipline, the conjuncture embraced by the accompaniment of music and the integrating effects of musical metaphors. The whole verbal pattern attempts to effect that difficult transition from personal love to political aspiration. But the experiment fails, simply because naturalistic narrative cannot contain such simultaneous diversity without exhibiting signs of strain. The difficulty has nothing to do with the supposed autonomy of individual emotion, or the supposed abstractness of political experience: the problem is aesthetic, not philosophical. In Warren Beatty's film *Reds* (1983), cinematic techniques accomplish an identical *montage* without difficulty: in a central sequence, shots of a marching crowd of revolutionaries singing the *Internationale* are inter-cut with shots of the 'private' tenderness of John Reed and Louise Bryant: the ambivalent separating/connecting effects of film-cutting effortlessly unify love and revolution into a single dimension – the strength of human love and solidarity, the excitement of love-making and struggle, the bliss of fulfilment and victory.

This judgement is not offered as a critical evaluation: we can do Jones's work more justice by reading it with an awareness of this tension between his revolutionary 'proletarian consciousness' and the constraints of the traditional naturalistic novel form. To read the novels solely as accurate imaginative accounts of real events is to privilege their naturalistic elements over their more experimental fictional interventions;[26] and moreover to render them unnecessarily vulnerable to the hostility of traditional novel criticism. Again, it is by employing devices of estrangement that Jones developed his fictional discourse to a point where it begins to challenge not only the traditional novel form, but the society that form reflects and largely endorses.

They both looked simultaneously past Len, and he, seeing their amaze-

[25]Lewis Jones, *We Live* (1939; London, Lawrence and Wishart, 1978), p. 139.
[26]Lewis Jones, Foreword to *Cwmardy* (1937; London, Lawrence and Wishart, 1978).

ment, turned his head to look in the same direction. He drew his breath sharply and his perspiring face went a shade whiter. The mountain which separated Cwmardy from the other valleys looked like a gigantic ant-hill, covered with a mass of black, waving bodies.

'Good God,' the man next to Mary whispered, 'the whole world is on the move' . . . she murmured: 'No, not yet. But the people are beginning to move it now.' . . . Len momentarily felt himself like a weak straw drifting in and out with the surge of bodies. Then something powerful swept through his being as the mass soaked its strength into him, and he realized that the strength of them all was the measure of his own, that his existence and power as an individual was buried in that of the mass now pregnant with motion behind him.[27]

As the mass moves into disciplined collective action, the very contours of the known world are defamiliarized: the mountain becomes a human shape, or an object now moveable by the application of collective strength and will. The absorption of the individual into the mass dispenses at once with traditional characterization and psychology: and the narrative prose, though deprived of so much of its former content, finds a new form and substance: though even here a dynamic, straining form, clamouring for the cinematic resources of visual imagery, poetic rhythm and aural accompaniment.

The specific historical situation of the Rhondda Valley in the 1920s and 30s, where Lewis Jones lived, worked and wrote, was capable of producing an image of class-struggle in the mining industry unrivalled in its clarity and simplicity. Although Jones consistently aligns the pattern of historical events not only with Marxist theory but with Communist Party policy, it would be an ignorant criticism that sought to allege any significant factual distortion. The strongly socialized nature of the Welsh mining community, intensified by contradictions of language and culture, could make a 'valley' and its 'people' a knowable political entity: in which the property-less class was sharply differentiated from the propertied; in which political confrontations tended to be immediate, physical and violent; in which powerful *local* loyalties could make for a radical solidarity of emotion and an absolute clarity of issue. In the course of the two novels the socially united and deeply interpersonal structure of the 'village' community is replaced by a society of collective solidarity and common unity, bound into harmony on the basis of Communist Party policy and programme. Again, in Welsh labour history there are specific local examples of such achievement: but as a *general* interpretation of *actual* history, the image could not withstand much serious interrogation. *We Live*, though it has some of the detail and complexity of actual history, resolves fictionally into the clarity and simplicity of myth: the powerful image of a possible future society, rather than an accurate record of a society that was.

[27]Jones, *We Live*, p. 243.

VI

The argument can be brought up to date by glancing briefly at the work of Barry Hines, native of a South Yorkshire mining village, who worked in the industry before becoming first teacher and then full-time writer. His best-known novel *A Kestrel for A Knave* (1968) (better-known by the title of the film adaptation *Kes*) is a proletarian novel still close in spirit to Lawrence as well as Brierley and the Sillitoe of *The Loneliness of the Long-Distance Runner*: the working-class community is perceived negatively by an alienated subject, Billy Caspar, representative of a humanity fiercely resist-ing incorporation into any of the available forms of social participa-tion – family, school, work (Billy will not follow his brother Jud down the pit), the law. As in Brierley, positive community is glimpsed only as an ideological fiction: at school Billy writes an idealized account of a happy family life, in response to the teacher's request for a 'tall story'. This lack of engagement with any experience of effective community renders all Billy's resistances wholly negative: petty pilfering, truancy, refusing the demands and appeals of mother, teacher, careers officer. Except, that is, his dis-covery of a positive oppositional energy in the fierce pride and indepen-dence of the kestrel he captures and trains. It is the *strangeness* of the kestrel that makes it, and the human responses sympathetic to it, capable of challenging a 'real world' all too familiar in its oppressive drudgery, casual brutality and irresponsible neglect.[28] After Jud has killed the hawk in an act of petty revenge, Billy enters a dimension of utter isolation and estrangement: sitting alone in a derelict cinema he fills an imagined screen with the contents of his own fantasy: re-enacting the drama of his father's leaving home, followed by a wish-fulfilment fantasy of potency and ven-geance, symbolized by the hawk:

> Big picture. Billy as hero. Billy on the screen. Big Billy. Kes on his arm. Big Kes. Close up. Technicolor. Looking round, looking down on them all, fierce-eyed. Audience murmuring. Billy in the audience, looking round at them all, proud. Billy casting Kes off, flying low, one rapid wide circuit, then gaining height, ringing up, hovering and sliding sideways a few yards, then ringing up to her pitch and waiting on while Billy walks forward. Jud breaks from cover, running hard through the heather. Kes sees him and stoops, breathtaking stoop, audience gasps. Too fast! Must be too fast. Picture blurring. No contact.   (159)

Prose breaks into film to disclose this fantasy, which is rather a revelation of psychological truth than an escapist daydream: 'no contact' expresses both Billy's incapacity to smite his wrongdoers and his actual condition of com-plete social alienation, the loss of himself.

The novel here has reached a limit and entered a new aesthetic conjunc-ture: the interpenetration of literary discourse and the media of film and

[28]Barry Hines, *A Kestrel for a Knave* (London, Penguin, 1969), pp. 118–19.

television. As Barry Hines is both novelist and television playwright, his work offers a clear demonstration of this development; his other novel of mining life, *The Price of Coal* (1979), was written in both forms, and the novel bears distinct traces of that relationship. Narrative is pared down to bare essentials, using an episodic technique based on the significant juxtaposition of brief contrasting scenes. There is no authorial commentary: an invisible narrator has the utter impersonality of a television camera. Detailed characterization of the kind familiar in the traditional novel barely exists.

The novel is divided into two parts, the first of which (entitled ironically 'Meet the People') describes the impact on a colliery of an official visit by Prince Charles. The techniques of television situation comedy are used to satirize the absurdly lavish preparations undertaken by the colliery management, consisting of unprecedented cosmetic decoration and a system of ludicrously irrelevant protocol. The terse, anecdotal scenes harness the oppositional energies of working-class humour to create a systematic satirical perspective, rooted in a proud class-consciousness: 'If all this fuss is worth making', observes the central character Syd, 'it's worth making for us. It's us who work here and live here. It's us who sees it every day, and it should be our needs that come first, not His'.[29] At times the rapid inter-cutting of very brief episodes gives the prose an effect akin to cinematic *montage*, in which meaning is generated from the apparently arbitrary juxtaposition of random details.[30]

The second part bears the title 'Back to Reality'. The phrase is employed initially by Forbes the colliery manager, as he shows his staff some of his preparations for 'The Visit':

'Now then, let's get back to reality, shall we?'
They walked along the front of the office block and stopped outside the main entrance. A new notice had been fixed to the wall at the side of the doors. It said:

NO PERSONNEL
ALLOWED INSIDE
WEARING OVERALLS   (37)

The everyday endurance and peril of the miners, their class-conscious resentment and militant anger, are to the colliery manager invented grievances, irrelevant distractions from a 'reality' gratuitously conferred on the pit by the approach of 'Royalty'. But the manager's practical, common-sense ideology, and the form of 'reality' it constructs, are both exploded by an underground disaster. The inter-cutting device is used again to express the diverse simultaneous impressions of those involved in the explosion:

[29]Barry Hines, *The Price of Coal* (London, Penguin, 1982), p. 45.
[30]Op. cit., pp. 85–6.

Frank connected the power cables to the transformer and dropped the switch.

Syd was walking back up the tailgate with Alan to fetch another ring. He turned to face the terrible roar, saw a blue flash, was lifted by the burning blast of air.

Harry felt the ground shake, heard the rushing air, was knocked down by it.   (109)

The sobering 'reality' of the blast which kills five men challenges and politicizes the ideological fiction of the Royal Visit.

The novel's 'filmic' technique, with its non-naturalistic capacity for juxtaposition and montage, obviously claims to proffer an alternative conception of 'reality'. Barry Hines is well aware however that the visual media belong to a cultural apparatus which is itself responsible for promulgating a powerful and persuasive version of 'reality'; in the novel it is associated with the press:

When George Kay's body was brought out of the pit, it was surrounded by cameramen and reporters, who photographed the covered form, and asked the stretcher bearers questions as they carried it across the pit yard and to the baths for identification.

And later, after Mrs. Kay had identified her husband, they surrounded her as she left the baths, crying quietly. . . .   (126)

Barry Hines's class-conscious literary experiments are an achievement in themselves. Because they are politically *and* artistically progressive, they demonstrate and demand further needs, beyond formal innovation: for a socially responsible press, a democratically-controlled television medium, a people's film industry; as well as a socialist literature.

VII

Of course there are other forms of discourse besides the novel, some particularly important to this history: ballad and song, speech and pamphlet, documentary, oral history, video recording. And of course the novel, itself the offspring of bourgeois culture, imposes constraints on the expression of working-class socialist consciousness. But the novel, as I have shown, is an enormously flexible form which can be made into a site of ideological struggle: not by naturalizing the form, not by exorcizing the nightmares of the bourgeois imagination; but by adapting them to express a proletarian vision which can interrogate as well as present 'reality'. The bourgeois novelists, as well as the philosophers, have already interpreted the world; the point, however, is to change it.

Note

Life and Works

'Lewis Grassic Gibbon' was the pseudonym of James Leslie Mitchell, born 1901 and died 1935. Gibbon wrote under both his real and his assumed name, and his considerable literary output includes novels, books on exploration including a life of Mungo Park, essays and short stories. Two useful books about Gibbon are: Ian S Munro, *Leslie Mitchell : Lewis Grassic Gibbon* (Edinburgh, Oliver and Boyd, 1966) – which includes a full list of his works – and D. Young, *Beyond the Sunset: a Study of James Leslie Mitchell* (Aberdeen, Impulse Publications, 1973). The three books comprising *A Scots Quair* appeared separately in 1932, 1933, and 1934 published by Jarrolds (London), and the same company issued the first complete edition in 1946. The present Hutchinson edition is identical in text (but not in pagination) to this edition. Gibbon collaborated with Hugh Macdiarmid to produce *Scottish Scene* (London, Jarrolds, 1934). Macdiarmid wrote about Gibbon after the latter's death: 'Lewis Grassic Gibbon', in Denys Val Baker, ed., *Modern British Writing* (New York, Vanguard Press, 1947). In 1967 a collection of Gibbon's essays and short stories, including some from *Scottish Scene*, was published as *A Scots Hairst*, ed. Ian S. Munro (London, Hutchinson, 1967).

Criticism

Feminist readings, like feminists and pro-feminists, come in many shapes, forms and colours. The particular reading presented here is heavily influenced by works such as Adrienne Rich's *On Lies, Secrets and Silence* (London, Virago, 1980), Elaine Showalter's 'Towards a Feminist Poetics', in Mary Jacobus, ed., *Women Writing and Writing About Women* (London, Croom Helm, 1982), as well as qualified readings of such feminist classics as Kate Millett's *Sexual Politics* (London, Virago, 1970) and Elaine Showalter's *A Literature of their Own* (London, Virago, 1978). Similarly this reading borrows some ways of seeing and some ways of writing emerging in aspects of post-structuralist critical theory. The interested reader should see the excellent bibliography in Catherine Belsey's *Critical Practice* (London, Methuen, 1980), as well as work by Michel Foucault – in particular his *The Order of Things* (London, Tavistock, 1970) and his *The Archaeology of Knowledge* (London, Tavistock, 1972). Many of the essays in Lydia Sargent's *The Unhappy Marriage of Marxism and Feminism* (London, Pluto Press, 1981) are contingently relevant, whereas, epistemologically speaking, Anthony Wilden's *System and Structure: Essays in Communication and Exchange* (London, Tavistock, 1972) and Fritjof Copra's *The Turning Point: Science Society and the Rising Culture* (London, Wildwood House, 1982) are centrally relevant.

3

A Feminist Reading of Lewis Grassic Gibbon's *A Scots Quair*[1]

Deirdre Burton

Reading Lewis Grassic Gibbon's famous trilogy in the early 1980s, I found I was having to remind myself continually that I was *not* reading a work by a modern female writer, who wrote from women's cultural experience, and with a strong political commitment to specifically feminist perspectives on major socialist issues. The aspects of the text that triggered this reaction in me were of various types, were to be found at varying levels, and ranged from the relatively slight and incidental (such as young Chris's reaction to reading *What Katy Did at School* – a remarkably insightful recognition of what that book, and others like it, have meant in the acculturation processes of many female readers), to the substantial and pervasive (such as the contradictory interrelations between the discourses of religion and sexuality throughout the three novels).

I want to use this article to focus on two of the more substantial issues my reading finds of interest. The first is a matter of representation, and some of the ways in which Gibbon manages to constitute a recognizably female 'reality' for and through Chris. The second concerns the political interpretation of the work as a whole, where I will be arguing that Gibbon offers extremely complex contradictions in the political positions taken by the characters in whom we are most interested, and, in the end, invites precisely those criticisms of the traditional Left as do modern feminist polemicists.

There are many ways in which *Sunset Song, Cloud Howe* and *Grey Granite* represent 'reality' with recognizably 'feminine' and profeminist biases, when the text coincides with Chris's developing consciousness. By this, I mean we find topics, attitudes, and techniques of representation that would, characteristically, dominate in other works of modern fiction written to be read as consciously feminist texts. So we find, for example,

---

[1]Please note that this is only 'a' feminist reading, and not by any means 'the' feminist reading. Not only are there as many feminist readings as there are feminisms, there are probably as many feminist readings as there are women.

features such as supportive friendships between women, both at critical times and in everyday life; the overt acknowledgement of the dependence of marriage on economic relations; dialogues between married couples which make strange the gender differences in their social relations with other people, and so on. In all such cases, Gibbon demonstrates himself to be remarkably sensitive to, and aware of, emergent feminist dilemmas and practices, in a way that many contemporary men and women were not. One feature of the text that stands out above and beyond all such specifics however, is the recurrent representation of Chris's awareness of her own split subjectivity and contradictory social and psychological positions.[2] There are four main devices that Gibbon uses in doing this. I will describe each of these briefly, and then discuss the implications of the use of them in the context of my reading of the work overall.

Firstly, there is the overt recognition and declaration of different identities – the simple existence of two or more selves. One substantial contradiction we find early on is the split between the 'English' Chris, who is to be educated, and find a career as a teacher away from the land, and the 'Scottish' Chris who belongs with the people of the crofting community:

> So that was the college place at Duncairn, two Chrisses went there each morning, and one was right douce and studious and the other sat back and laughed a canny laugh at the antics of the teachers and minded Blawearie brae and the champ of horses and the smell of dung and her father's brown, grained hands till she was sick to be home again.[3]   (45)

This contradiction is, at first, one that Chris seems to impose on herself though, clearly, it is a distinction she has learned from the discourses around her. It recurs frequently, but as she and the text progress, the social nature of the national and class distinction becomes clearer:

> And Chris would stand in the choir and sing, and sometimes look at the page in her hand and think of the days when she at Blawearie had never thought of the kirk at all, overbusied living the life that was *now* to bother at all on the life to come. Others of the choir that had missed a service would say to her with a shy-like smile, *I'm so sorry, Mrs. Coloquohoun, I was late*; and Chris would say that they needn't fash, if she said it in Scots the woman would think *Isn't that a common-like bitch at the Manse*? If she said it in English, the speak would spread round the minister's wife was putting on airs.   (209)

---

[2] I am here referring to the Lacanian concept of the split subject, and, by implication, the discussion of the concept in recent critical theory. Jacques Lacan, *The Four Fundamental Concepts of Psychoanalysis*, trans. Alan Sheridan (London, Hogarth Press, 1977).
[3] All references are to the following edition: Lewis Grassic Gibbon, *A Scots Quair* (2nd, reset, printing London, Hutchinson, 1974; it contains *Sunset Song*, pp. 11–194; *Cloud Howe*, pp. 195–351; and *Grey Granite*, pp. 353–496).

Similarly Chris acquires multiple identities as she marries and moves on through three marriages, pregnancy, child-birth, a miscarriage and beyond. Sometimes this seems a relatively simple cumulative development, sometimes the taking of a new name brings with it an apparent transformation:

> She felt neither gladness nor pain, only dazed, as though running in the fields with Ewan she had struck against a great stone, body and legs and arms, and lay stunned and bruised, the running and the fine crying in the sweet air still on about her, Ewan running fee and careless still not knowing or heeding the thing she had met. The days of love and holidaying and the foolishness of kisses – they might be for him yet but never the same for her, dreams were fulfilled and their days put by, the hills climbed still to sunset but her heart might climb with them never again and long for to-morrow, the night still her own. No night would she ever be her own again, in her body the seed of that pleasure she had sown with Ewan burgeoning and growing, dark, in the warmth below her heart. And Chris Guthrie crept out from the place below the beech trees where Chris Tavendale lay and went wandering off into the waiting quiet of the afternoon, Chris Tavendale heard her go, and she came back to Blaewearie never again.   (137)

A second recurrent means of representing Chris's split self, which appears in the passage just quoted, as in numerous other places, is the syntactical technique whereby her body parts take on grammatical and ideational subject functions in their own right, and as markedly distinct from Chris's body or body/mind as a whole unit. Another example may help to clarify this:

> And then it was she found no salvation at all may endure for ever, or beyond the pitch that the heart may bear it, she was weeping and weeping, her arms flung over the kitchen table, weeping for that Ewan who had never come back, for the shamed, tormented boy with the swagger airs she had let go from Blawearie without a kiss or a parting word. *Ewan, Ewan*! her heart cried then, breaking and breaking, *Oh, Ewan, I didn't mean it*! Ewan – he was hers, hers still in spite of all he had done and said, he had lived more closely in her body than the heart that broke now. . . .   (173)

A third frequently recurring feature, closely related to this, is a technique which again separates the whole Chris from her body parts, by constituting them as objects of her gaze, functioning syntactically as grammatical objects in clauses where 'she' is the grammatical subject and so, in contrast to the previous examples, semantically and syntactically dominant to the body parts:

> She thought that cool and unwarmed, still in the grip of the strange

white dreaming that had been hers, looking down at herself naked as though she looked at some other than herself, a statue like that of the folk of olden times that they set in the picture galleries. And she saw the light white on the satin of her smooth skin then, and the long smooth lines that lay from waist to thigh, thigh to knee, and was glad her legs were long from the knee to the ankle, that made legs seem stumbling and stumpy, shortness there. And still impersonally she bent to see if that dimple still hid there under her left breast, it did, it was deep as ever. Then she straightened and took down her hair and brushed it, standing so, silly to stand without her night-gown, but that was the mood she was in, somehow it seemed that never again would she be herself, have this body that was hers and her own, those fine lines that curved from thigh to knee hers, that dimple she'd loved when a child – oh years before!   (116)

The fourth recurring device which perforce incorporates similar syntactic features, is that of presenting Chris regarding her own image in a mirror, or in water reflections of some sort. As in all the other cases, examples are numerous – it appears to be a process she enters at any time of crisis or change:

It was bright and warm in the room, she turned round and saw her lad sit so; and then she raised her head and saw herself in the long, old mirror of the parlour wall, and thought how she'd changed, it crept on you and you hardly noticed, in ways you were still as young as the quean with the plaits that had run by Marget to catch the scholar's train. But she saw herself then in her long green skirt, long under the knee, and her hair wound in its great fair plaits about her head, and her high cheek-bones that caught the light and her mouth that was well enough, her figure was better still; and she knew for one wild passing moment herself both frightened and sorry she should be a woman, she'd never dream things again, she'd live them, the days of dreaming were by; and maybe they had been the best. . . .   (113)

It is impossible in an article this length to give a sense of how often these features recur and how dominant they are. The point I want to bring out though, is the surprise at finding them having so axiomatic a place in a novel not usually classified specifically as pro-feminist writing. In both poetry and prose by women, and certainly in explicitly feminist work, but also in work not consciously conceptualized as such,[4] such features and devices are absolutely commonplace – almost an identifying characteristic of women's writing in this century. What is surprising, and impressive, here is Gibbon's sympathetic sense of the massive centrality of the

[4]See my articles: Deirdre Burton, 'Through Glass Darkly: Through Dark Glasses', in R.A. Carter, ed., *Language and Literature: An Introductory Reader in Stylistics* (London, George Allen & Unwin, 1982), pp. 195–217, and Deirdre Burton, 'Pulling Yourself Together: Images of the split subject in women's writing' (University of Birmingham, mimeo, 1983).

dilemma of contradictory subject positions in female experience. It is seldom far from Chris's consciousness – or ours.

Jenny Wolmark's interesting article 'Problems of Tone in *A Scots Quair*',[5] provides a convenient starting point for my second topic. She argues against a simple and reductive appraisal of the trilogy just as an outstanding socialist prose work, and examines the contradictory presence of socialist and liberal ideology in the text, as a way of understanding the hegemonic crisis in monopoly capitalism in the years between the world wars. She points to the conflicts and contradictions that are revealed in the text (and in the dominant ideology) by referring to the basic narrative structure of the trilogy:

> This can be demonstrated by looking at the narrative structure of *A Scots Quair*, which is organized around the central metaphor of the journey undertaken by the two main characters in the trilogy – Chris, a crofter's daughter, and her son Ewan. During the course of the trilogy, they move from a peasant community of Scottish crofters, to a semi-industrialized town, and finally to an industrial city. The journey acts as a metaphor for the historical process which encompasses the destruction of the peasant community and the emergence of the militant working class in the 1930s. During the course of the journey, Ewan is radicalized, becomes a Communist, and joins the Hunger Marchers. Chris, however, rejects her son's radical politics, gives up all contact with him, and returns, alone, to the farm where she was born. The trilogy ends at that point, and no attempt is made within the narrative to reconcile the different experiences and beliefs of Chris and Ewan. So the narrative structure presents two contradictory perspectives on that historical process: on the one hand, it offers a radical and positive criticism of capitalism by focussing on the growth of Ewan's political consciousness. On the other hand, it presents a profoundly conservative idealization of the past and a fatalistic acceptance of history as something to be endured rather than understood.

It is an article I respect in many ways, but, in the extract just quoted, I find myself at odds with her conclusions. From what I had read about Gibbon's trilogy in cultural histories of the thirties, I had been expecting a text that would present and endorse a relatively uncomplicated support for the working class and the Communist Party. However, I didn't, and couldn't, find that at all, or not in any simple way. Now, clearly, this is in part a product of my interests and political biases before I came to the text – no reading can be innocent or free from its reader's presuppositions. On the other hand, I had been prepared to read it as a political document of the thirties, and was fully interested in seeing how this famous text of the

[5]Jenny Wolmark, 'Problems of Tone in *A Scots Quair*', *Red Letters* 11 (1981), pp. 15–23.

proletariat would depict and support the contemporary extremist point of view. It was a very real surprise, then, to find the novels doing something quite different. For, though they clearly describe the nature and extent of the oppression of the working class, they also do not suggest that the mobilized Left have anything like an adequate vision with which to transform existing power relations.[6] I will try to clarify and ground this reading position by referring first of all to Jenny Wolmark's final sentence. I will then add some points that relate more closely to women's politics and specific criticisms of overlapping gender-blindness in traditional Marxism and patriarchy.

Firstly, then, it does not seem to me that the text allows us to focus 'equally' on Ewan and Chris and their different political consciousnesses. The structural evidence is such that Chris is a much more predominant filter for both events and opinions, as, firstly her developing consciousness holds our attention for a significantly greater amount of time (Ewan does not really compete for our attention till one third of the way through the final novel). Secondly, the fact that the trilogy *closes* with her point of view, undoubtedly suggests that hers is a vision to be endorsed, when all is said and done. I am not suggesting that this was Gibbon's 'intention', of course – I suspect he may well have had notions of symmetry, or closure with the overtly poetic in mind here, but, given the influence of framing devices and poetic closures in general reading experience, it is hard to leave the trilogy without a sense that Chris's vision – liberal, and a refusal of direct radicalism as it may be – is none the less the more powerful and all-encompassing. Similarly, it is Chris with whom we have learned to sympathize, and whom we have watched with admiration as she advances through adolescence and maturity. This has not been an uncritical admiration, for the text makes quite clear her mistakes and her misconceptions, as well as her developing integrity, which is inescapably a part of the text, that again suggests to me that Chris and Ewan are not drawn with equal voice or power for the reader. I will return to this below, in a more detailed discussion of Ewan's presentation, but let me mention here an interesting connected detail.

One of the strengths of the work is its refusal to idealize anyone or anything – so that the reader has a sense of a particularly honest representation of the various communities involved in the narrative. What is interesting, though, is the number and distribution of characters endorsed with integrity. Chris, certainly, and throughout the three books, is an object of our admiration in this respect – though not above making mistakes, and not beyond criticism. In the first novel, Chae Strachan and Long Rob, in their different ways, come across quite clearly and strongly as equally admirable. There is then a substantial absence, throughout the second novel, with Chris herself carrying the weight of the only really reliable

---

[6]I use 'transform' deliberately here, following Adrienne Rich's criticisms of the patriarchal connotations of the word 'revolution'. See Adrienne Rich, 'Power and Danger: works of a Common Woman', in her collection *On Lies, Secrets, Silence* (London, Virago, 1980), pp. 247–59.

point of view – whilst Robert flickers and dims, and young Ewan begins to glimmer. In the final novel, despite a tremendous surge of possibility and potential in Ewan, eventually he too behaves without integrity at a personal level – in his compromises with Party propaganda, in his treatment of Ellen – and we are left with a sense of three women, Chris, Ellen, and Ma Cleghorn (the latter in a quiet and understated way) as the people who are to be trusted in their dealings with others, despite their varying commitments to public politics – despite, even, their failures at that level.

Now, in many ways, it would be easy enough to dismiss observations and discussion of concepts like 'integrity' and 'honesty' in personal relationships as yet more liberalism. Fortunately for feminist-socialists, the slogan 'the personal is political' at least raises these issues as problematic, and suggests that they are not necessarily to be dismissed in politically oriented discussions. Whilst I could not, and would not want to argue that Gibbon was actively supporting this notion, it seems to me that the text invites this particular type of interrogation. In a fictional world where so many characters are offered as people to criticize in their interpersonal dealings, those few who contrast stand out quite clearly. In this respect too, then, it seems to me that we do not focus equally on Chris and Ewan at all.

Now, as to whether Chris's view of the past is a 'conservative idealization' or not, it would be hard to argue that her vision is in any way a recognizably radical one. On the other hand, it is more complex than that phrase would suggest, and is again not out of tune with certain groupings within the Women's Movement. It seems to be that Chris's alignment with the past is really an identification with place, and the organic community. It is characterized by a mystical resonance with times past, complete with visions of the dead, profound sensitivity to the magnetism of the Standing Stones, and an overall (and often repeated) sense of personal transience:

> And then a queer thought came to her there in the drooked fields, that nothing endured at all, nothing but the land she passed across, tossed and turned and perpetually changed below the hands of the crofter folk since the oldest of them had set the Standing Stones by the loch of Blaewearie and climbed there on their holy days and saw their terraced crops ride brave in the wind and the sun. Sea and sky and the folk who wrote and fought and were learnéd, teaching and saying and praying, they lasted but as a breath, a mist of fog in the hills, but the land was forever, it moved and changed below you, but was forever, you were close to it and it to you, not at a bleak remove it held you and hurted you. And she had thought to leave it all!   (97)

The context for this particular extract is that of Chris, after her father's death, planning to leave Blaewearie and follow an education and career in Aberdeen. A passage leading to the book's closure should perhaps be quoted here too:

Crowned with mists, Bennachie was walking into the night: and Chris moved and sat with her knees hand-clasped, looking far on that world across the plain and the day that did not die there but went east, on and on, over all the world till the morning somewhere on the world. No twilight land anywhere for shade, sun or night the portion of all, her little shelter in Cairndhu a dream of no-life that could not endure. And that was the best deliverance of all, as she saw it now, sitting here quiet – that that Change who ruled the earth and the sky and the waters underneath the earth, Change whose face she'd once feared to see, whose right hand was Death and whose left hand Life, might be stayed by none of the dreams of men, love, hate, compassion, anger or pity, gods or devils or wild crying to the sky. He passed and repassed in the ways of the wind, Deliverer, Destroyer and Friend in one.   (496)

Whilst there are many conventional ways of dismissing her feelings and experiences as merely conservative, sentimental, illogical and so on, recent writing and thinking not only permits a review of such condemnatory adjectives, but invites an understanding of those condemnations as revealing the biases and prejudices of specifically *patriarchal* values. I am thinking here of work which re-views the history of ideas from a feminist or pro-feminist perspective and which demonstrates the connections between so-called 'rationalist', or mechanistic paradigms and the interests of both capitalism and patriarchy together.[7]

They clearly ask for a re-evaluation of current value-judgements given to both 'masculine' (the logical, analytical, objective, rational) and 'feminine' (the intuitive, synthetic, subjective, mystical) ways of thinking. In this respect, there are many quotable instances in *Grey Granite* that show us where Ewan's taken-for-granted norms are:

Ellen said nothing for a little while and Ewan had half-forgotten her when she asked of a sudden: *Are you losing heart?*

He said *Eh*? and then *Oh, about capitalism? Losing heart would do a lot of good, wouldn't it?*

She said then something, queer kid, he was to remember: *Anyhow, your heart's not in it at all. Only your head and imagination.*

– And I'm not in much danger of losing either. You don't quarrel with History and its pace of change any more than you quarrel with the law of gravitation.   (414)

The new physics, although it does not, of course, deny the law of gravitation, certainly does offer a wider vision of the phenomenal world, and once that leap out of the Cartesian-Newtonian episteme has been made in that discipline, so too it can be made in all branches of knowledge; economics,

[7]See, for example, Carolyn Merchant, *The Death of Nature: Women, Ecology and the Scientific Revolution* (New York, Harper & Row, 1980).

history, sociology as well as biology, medicine, ecology.[8] The emergent paradigm accords neatly with what has traditionally been classified as 'feminine' ways of thinking. And Chris, far from merely removing herself from the immediate political action can be read as contributing to that shift in conceptualization that will require a different kind of political understanding and activity.

Again, I am not suggesting that Gibbon was somehow setting out to incorporate a modern feminist personal–political experiential cosmology, but the text is unbelievably rich in such insights and possible readings, and we are *not* encouraged to dismiss Chris as weak-minded or precious in any way. Certainly, history is not 'understood', in the sense that it is *analysed*, yet somehow Chris has knowledge, wisdom of something beyond the confines of both capitalism and patriarchy.

Let me return to the presentation of Ewan, and whether or not our sympathies are unproblematically with him. There are many instances, certainly, in the final novel, where he does surely invite our wholehearted support. At the end of the New Year's Eve dance, for example

> And as they cheered him and cried his name, the dirty, kind words of mates in the Shops, a great chap that Ewan, just one of themselves . . . again, he'd never be ought but a bit of them, the flush on a thin white mill-girl's face, the arm and hand and the downbent face of a keelie from the reek of the Gallowgate, the blood and bones and flesh of them all, their thoughts and their doubts and their loves were his, all that they thought and lived in were his.   (430; my ellipsis, D.B.)

Or in his conversion first to Socialism and then to Communism, and his unquestioning and absolute commitment. Surely, too, the inclusion of the hideous torture he receives from the police – whether or not he had been justly accused – is designed to engage our sympathies entirely, and enduringly. The case, as ever in these novels, is not so simple.

To take the last mentioned incident – an initial reaction to these disgusting and shameful scenes is a simple one whereby the reader takes sides: for Ewan; against the police. But, in fact, something the text as a whole refuses absolutely is the easy taking of sides. Consider, say, the presentation of Chris's parents – consistently (at first) we seem to be invited to side with Mrs Guthrie against her husband. Every dialogue shows his illtemper, her hardship, his cruelty, her patience. And yet, later reflections about them suggest criticism of her – sympathetic criticism, but criticism none the less, and sympathy for him – victims both of them.

Similarly, with many of the country or town characters who appear, we are asked to accept all sorts of contradictory evidence about them, and asked to acknowledge changing opinions of them. Apropos the physical violence of the police and what seems to be a very simple resolution of

[8]See Fritjof Capra, *The Turning Point: Science, Society and the Rising Culture* (London, Wildwood House, 1982).

right- and wrong-doers, consider the contradictory evidence of *Sunset Song*, where the class with whom our sympathies lie are also depicted as inflicting excessive and sadistic physical violence on a helpless victim. In this case the recipient is 'daft' Andy, who has, certainly, run away and frightened a couple of women – though never in anything but a rather pathetic way – the fear being lodged in his queerness, not in any actual threat.

> Feint the thing else he'd to eat that day, he was near the end of his tether; for though he ran like a hare and Cuddiestoun behind him was more than coarse in the legs, yet luck would have it that Mutch of Bridge End was just guiding his team across the road to start harrowing his yavil park when the two runners came in sight, real daft-like both of them, Andy running near double, soap and madness a-foam on his face. Cuddiestoun bellowing behind.
>
> So Mutch slowed down his team and called out to Andy, *Ay, man, you mustn't run near as fast as that*, and when Andy opposite threw out a foot and tripped him up, and down in the stour went Andy and Cuddiestoun was on top of him in a minute, bashing in the face of him, but Alex Mutch just stood and looked on, maybe working his meikle ears a bit, it was no concern of his. The daftie's hands went up to his face as the bashings came and then Cuddiestoun gripped him in a tender private part, he screamed and went slack, like a sack in Cuddiestoun's arms.   (51)

Here, as elsewhere, Gibbon is refusing absolutely the possibility of simplifying human actions, morals, ethics. He makes similarly problematic the behaviour and strategies of the Keelies (the working men) throughout *Grey Granite*, to the point where central figures in the local Communist party are not only dishonest as a political strategy, but ill-treat friends, and even abscond with Party funds.

The final scene between Ewan and Ellen creates still more obstacles in the way of an easy alignment with Ewan's ways of thinking and his actions. Certainly, Ellen is selling out politically. The education authorities have threatened to dismiss her from her teaching job unless she removes herself from extremist activities. She has capitulated and signed a document to that effect. Worse still, in this sense, she wants to move into a world of possessions, money, self-interest, a settled family life. In many ways, she is presented critically, therefore. Nevertheless she is the person who introduced Ewan to socialism in the first place, she is the person who has consistently offered him her love and support, who helped him through a mental and physical crisis after the police torture, who has remained honest in all her dealings with other people. She does not, it seems to me, deserve the treatment she gets from Ewan. Nor is it even a constructive political strategy on his part, since clearly it is designed to dismiss her from the Party entirely:

He stood up then, dark and slim, still a boy, and brushed her off carefully, and the snow from his knees: *Go to them then in your comfortable car - your Labour Party and your comfortable flat. But what are you doing out here with me? I can get a prostitute anywhere.*

She sat still, bloodless, could only whisper: *Ewan!*

He stood looking at her coolly, not angered, called her a filthy name, consideringly, the name a keelie gives to a leering whore; and turned and walked down the hill from her sight.   (490)

It is that recourse to the irrelevant insults of sexuality that finally marks Ewan out as the person of limited vision, limited growth – both personal and political. With that recognition comes the recollection and understanding of the ways in which patriarchal attitudes have consistently excluded women, their experiences, their insights, their work from all radical movements and activities except their own.[9]

It is easy to see why *A Scots Quair* is often just referred to in passing in books about culture, politics and literature of the period.[10] Its complexity and contradictions, and its problematic refusal to idealize the man who should somehow have been the 'hero' of this proletarian novel, make it a difficult text to reconcile politically in any traditional straightforward and unqualified way. On the other hand, in the current climate – and I am here thinking quite specifically of the differences between Marxisms and feminisms – these complexities and contradictions render it a powerfully radical interrogative text. Heidi Hartmann states the current crisis clearly enough:[11]

> the 'marriage' of marxism and feminism has been like that between husband and wife depicted in common law: marxism and feminism are one, and that one is marxism. Recent attempts to integrate marxism and feminism are unsatisfactory to us as feminists because they subsume that feminist struggle into the 'larger' struggle against capital. To continue our simile further, either we need a healthier marriage, or we need a divorce.
>
> The inequalities in this marriage, like most social phenomena, are no accident. Many marxists typically argue that feminism is at best less important than class conflict, and at worst divisive of the working class. This political stance produces an analysis that absorbs feminism into the class struggle. Moreover, the analytical power of marxism with respect to capital has obscured its limitations with respect to sexism.

It may well be that the realist novel itself – its structure and its necessary

[9]See, for example, Lydia Sargent, ed., *The Unhappy Marriage of Marxism and Feminism* (London, Pluto Press, 1981).

[10]See Jon Clark, Margot Heinemann, David Margolies and Carol Snee, *Culture and Crisis in Britain in the 1930s* (London, Lawrence & Wishart, 1979), and Frank Gloversmith, ed., *Class, Culture and Social Change* (Brighton, Harvester Press, 1980).

[11]Heidi Hartmann, 'The Unhappy Marriage of Marxism and·Feminism: towards a more progressive union', in Sargent, *Marriage*, pp. 1–43.

ideational content – render it a form incompatible with an unproblematic radical politics that *could* exclude a female point of view. The quality of the trilogy that allows it to be radical in terms of sexual as well as class politics is, however, that it foregrounds the female point of view, and in that way contributes to an understanding of history beyond the limitations of patriarchy.

Note

Love on the Dole was first published in 1933 by Jonathan Cape, and has subsequently run into many editions; it is currently in print as a Penguin Modern Classic. It has been translated and published abroad in various countries from Russia to Israel, and is the best known of Walter Greenwood's works although he has had another 10 novels published as well as a collection of short stories, several plays and a book of personal reminiscences, *There Was a Time* (1967).

Walter Greenwood was born in 1903 and spent his childhood in Salford in the Hankinson Street area, the 'Hanky Park' of *Love on the Dole*. He left school at 13, having already worked part-time in a pawnshop and as a milkroundsman's boy, and took a variety of jobs and spent several periods unemployed before *Love on the Dole* was accepted for publication in 1932 after an earlier novel had been turned down. He died in 1974.

Love on the Dole was extremely popular in the 1930s, running into three impressions in the first year of publication alone. Its popularity as a novel was enhanced by a stage version, written by Ronald Gow, a Manchester playwright; this was first performed in 1934 and published in 1935.

There is not a great deal of literary criticism on *Love on the Dole*, and virtually none on Greenwood's other works. Most of the recent criticism has tended to be rather hostile and I have considered some of the issues raised in the following discussion of the novel. The fullest account is by Stephen Constantine who considers the historical context and impact of the novel: his article and other works which discuss or mention *Love on the Dole* are referred to below and referenced in the footnotes. The University of Salford has a collection of Walter Greenwood papers, including many press cuttings and the shooting script for the film of the novel which was released in 1941.

4

Love on the Dole and the Aesthetic of Contradiction

Roger Webster

In the year of its publication, 1933, *Love on the Dole* received an apprecia-
tive review in *The Times Literary Supplement*: 'as a novel it stands very
high, but it is in its qualities as a "social document" that its great value
lies' stated the reviewer before outlining the plot.[1] Later reviews in the
1930s of the novel and the dramatic version which followed were similarly
enthusiastic, praising its realist qualities. Yet in spite of its continuous
appeal to a wide audience from the time of publication, academic responses to the novel have not been frequent or favourable. Of the literary
criticism on the 1930s, three major works do not mention *Love on the Dole*
in spite of its popular status as a quintessential work of the decade.[2] The
English academic establishment has been conspicuously reluctant to
embrace the work or its author; there is no major critical study to date of
Greenwood's writing though he has published some 10 novels in addition
to *Love on the Dole* as well as several plays and a book of short stories. It is
equally anomalous that although Greenwood has been considered by
literary critics as a founder of the working-class or proletarian novel, he has
been accorded less attention than some of his successors. The volume of
critical work on Alan Sillitoe considerably outweighs that on Greenwood,
yet Sillitoe has acknowledged Greenwood, stating in 1978, 'The whole
proletarian movement in literature before the war or between the wars
really failed – with the possible exception of Walter Greenwood's *Love on
the Dole*, which was a good book.'[3] The authors of two recent articles
which have discussed the novel in the context of working-class literature
and proletarian writing have attacked Greenwood for propagating middle-
class values and retaining unquestioningly the bourgeois form of fiction,

[1]Mrs. D.L. Murray, review of *Love on the Dole* by Walter Greenwood, in *The Times Literary
Supplement* (29 June 1933). The same review was reprinted in the *TLS* (1 July 1983).
[2]The works in question are: Bernard Bergonzi, *Reading the Thirties* (London, Macmillan,
1978); Samuel Hynes, *The Auden Generation* (London, Bodley Head, 1976); Julian Symons,
The Thirties: A Dream Revolved (London, Faber, 1960). Professor Bergonzi has subsequently
acknowledged the importance of *Love on the Dole* in an article entitled 'Myths of the
Thirties', *The Times Higher Educational Supplement* (19 March 1982).
[3]John Halperin, 'Interview with Alan Sillitoe', *Modern Fiction Studies* 25:2 (1979), p. 178.

that of the traditional realist novel. Roy Johnson, whilst recognizing documentary and historical qualities, argues that 'many of the values it holds highest are those of polite middle-class orthodoxy.'[4] Carole Snee perceives a discrepancy between the novel's overrated public reception and status – now reprinted as a Penguin Modern Classic – and 'its impact as a text when read'.[5] She goes on to state, 'Greenwood may have been a working-class novelist, writing about working-class life, but he never challenges the form of the bourgeois novel, nor its underlying ideology.' Ramón López Ortega has given a brief but more favourable account of the novel, defending one of the central characters, Larry Meath, though he suggests that Greenwood's prose is 'contrived' at times.[6]

The most comprehensive critical account of the novel is by an historian, Stephen Constantine,[7] and generally it has received more attention from historians than literary critics; Arthur Marwick, A.J.P. Taylor, and Noreen Branson and Margot Heinemann have all treated *Love on the Dole* as an important documentary work.[8] Constantine argues persuasively about the results of the novel's impact on the historical consciousness of the middle classes, especially in the south of England, suggesting that it 'worked in the opposite direction' to the general pattern of movement on the literary map of the thirties with the norm being excursions by writers of middle-class background such as George Orwell or J.B. Priestley to the working-class North: 'it brought the North to the South'. He contends that in order to penetrate southern middle-class consciousness Greenwood adopted a strategy which would not offend the readership: there is no portrayal of 'middle-class villains, personifying the enemy of the working class and the cause of their distress.' The General Strike of 1926 is not mentioned and experience is presented from a series of individual points of view, aspects which Johnson and Snee had already considered as defects in the novel. Constantine is tentative about any putative effects of *Love on the Dole* on social consciousness and policy towards the end of the thirties and subsequently, with the qualification that 'though historians can hardly weigh imponderables, it would be inaccurate as a consequence to discount them entirely'.

As Snee and Johnson have argued, the plot of *Love on the Dole* is an aspect of the text that is strongly foregrounded, which is in keeping with

[4]Roy Johnson, 'The Proletarian Novel', *Literature and History* 2:2 (1975), p. 88.
[5]Carole Snee, 'Working-Class Literature or Proletarian Writing?', in John Clark, Margot Heinemann, David Margolies and Carole Snee, eds., *Culture and Crisis in Britain in the Thirties* (London, Lawrence and Wishart, 1979), p. 170.
[6]Ramón López Ortega, 'The language of the working-class novel of the 1930s', in H. Gustav Klaus, ed., *The Socialist Novel in Britain: Towards the Recovery of a Tradition* (Brighton, Harvester, 1982), p. 128.
[7]Stephen Constantine, '*Love on the Dole* and its Reception in the 1930s', *Literature and History* 8:2 (1982).
[8]Arthur Marwick, *Britain in the Century of Total War* (London, Penguin, 1970), p. 238. A.J.P. Taylor, *English History: 1914–1945* (London, Penguin, 1970), p. 436. Noreen Branson and Margot Heinemann, *Britain in the Nineteen Thirties* (St Albans, Granada, 1973), p. 292.

the realist convention. The main action turns on the central character, Harry Hardcastle, with his changing fortunes from working as a half-time clerk in Price and Jones's pawnshop to an apprenticeship at Marlowe's engineering works, unemployment and eventual re-employment on the city buses. There is also a relationship between Harry and a factory-girl, Helen, which blossoms when they manage to afford a holiday with Harry's winnings on a horse-bet; they marry subsequently when Helen becomes pregnant even though this involves Harry's being turned out of his parents' home and the couple's living in squalid conditions at Helen's parents' house. Harry is clearly individualized, as to a lesser degree are other characters central to the plot and action: Harry's sister Sally Hardcastle, and Larry Meath – an educated factory worker who acts as a spokesman for the working class and socialism in the tradition of the autodidact (in particular the main character of Robert Tressell's *The Ragged Trousered Philanthropists*, Owen). The individualism of these figures though is set against forms of a more collective social awareness, the characters oscillating between their individual status and an amorphous, impersonal world of mass unemployment. Harry eventually sees himself as 'a unit of the spectral army of three million lost men' after his self-delusion about the heroic life of operating a machine has disintegrated.

Although experience is frequently presented in the novel from a series of individual points of view, I intend to show that such perceptions are questioned and subverted within the text. The process of normalization or naturalization which inheres in the bourgeois ideology of the realist novel, operating largely through the constructions of individual characters and plot, is clearly foregrounded and mythicized in *Love on the Dole* in a manner that reveals rather than obscures its contradictions. The 'truth' produced may be, at one level, documentary in that the work appears to be a faithful reproduction of aspects of working-class life in the 1930s, but the text also acknowledges its ability to create illusions and indicates its own fictionality; as Pierre Macherey has commented, fiction 'can set illusion in motion by penetrating its insufficiency, by transforming our relationship to ideology. . . . Fiction deceives us in so far as its is feigned; but this is not a primary act of deception, because it is aimed at one even more profound, exposing it, helping to release us from it.'[9] It is in the relationship and alliance between bourgeois ideology in fiction and in capitalist society that *Love on the Dole* produces significant and problematic issues. It will be argued that its narrative structure is not purposive and progressive, unlike that of the classic realist novel whose plot and action are directed towards an affirmation of conventional values by asserting unquestioningly individualized experience and maintaining illusions through silences and artificial reconciliations of social and psychological contradictions in the plausible persona of a particular case. As Snee has remarked, the traditional realist novel uses a narrative pattern which 'begins with the

[9]Pierre Macherey, *A Theory of Literary Production* (London, Routledge & Kegan Paul, 1978), p. 64.

individual, moves out into the social world, and finally back into the individual consciousness'.

Love on the Dole begins not with an individual, but a panoramic view of Hanky Park.[10] The dominant features are its general characteristics; the narrative voice is impersonal and detached, the repeated use of pronouns suggesting the anonymous, invisible forces and relations of power which manipulate the occupants of Hanky Park and the text: 'They call this "Hanky Park" ', ' "crofts" as they are called'; humanity is merely intimated as 'the traffic of boots and clogs'. The images of erosion – the streets polished by feet, the flag-paved floors of houses being continually scoured – combined with the view of the industrial landscape as 'nude black patches of land', the pavements having 'a distant resemblance to a patchwork quilt', create the sense of a dehumanized, fragmented and alien world with the incongruous figurative language of 'mazes' and 'jungles' echoing similar descriptions in Dickens's *Hard Times*. The scene is insidious, humanity submerged in the smoke from 'a million squat chimneys', as indistinguishable from their environment as 'the cotton and humanity' from which the businessmen had made their 'millions'. The second chapter of Part One opens with the documentary style more generally associated with the novel:

5.30 A.M.
   A drizzle was falling.
   The policeman on his beat paused awhile at the corner of North Street halting under a street lamp. Its staring beams lit the million globules of fine rain powdering his cape. A cat sitting on the doorstep of Mr Hulkington's, the grocer's shop, blinked sleepily.
   'Tsh-tsh-tsh-tsh-tsh,' said the bobby and stopped to scratch the animal's head. It rose, crooked its back, cocked its tail, pushed its body against his hand and miowed.
   The melancholy hoot of a ship's siren sounded from the Salford Docks.

Humanity in individual form first appears in the figure of the anonymous policeman. The physical setting still retains its indifferent, amorphous aspect, the isolated units of life are absorbed into the material vastness. An innumerable immensity is suggested again by the 'million globules of fine rain'. Numerical language is reiterated throughout the text, isolated figures being juxtaposed with vast numbers, which indicates the contradiction of the perception of the individual as subject apparently set apart from the thousands or millions of 'human pygmies', 'ants', or the 'army' which compose society. Harry's naïve pride on first joining Marlowe's works – 'And they'd given him a number, 2510. There was the hallmark of his engagement' – is an ironic reflection of an early stage in the process of his loss of identity and self-respect as a working man.

[10]Walter Greenwood, *Love on the Dole* (London, Penguin, 1969). All quotations are taken from this edition.

The Hardcastle family is introduced later in this chapter and Harry's thoughts are presented in a crude form of interior monologue, a narrative mode which is the most extreme expression of subjective individualism. There is, though, a tension or inconsistency between Harry's inner and outer presentation, as with other characters presented in this manner. The transcription of Harry's thoughts is not in dialect, whereas his spoken words are. As we shall see, there is a disjuncture between his psychological and social identities which is further reflected in the inconsistency of the narrative discourses. What might be considered as an authorial intervention, a logical weakness and aesthetic flaw can be alternatively read as a significant break in the illusion created by the fiction of the text. On the one hand, Greenwood's recourse to a bourgeois literary language makes Harry's thoughts more accessible to the reader, especially if intended for a Southern middle-class audience. (Some of the expressions in dialect are 'translated' as Constantine has pointed out. This is an aspect of a significantly different treatment of language by Greenwood from that of proletarian writers such as Lewis Grassic Gibbon.) On the other hand, the location of this discourse within a range of contradictory linguistic registers ascribed to characters and the world beyond is not so much a way of making sense of their situation but rather of indicating the nature of their imprisonment within a bourgeois and bourgeois-literary ideology. It is one of the ways in which the text can be seen to question its own realism: the inconsistencies fracture the convention of mimetic realism in order to indicate tensions which reside in a world beyond the formal demands and constraints of linguistic consistency. The rhetoric of fictional style has its dissonant notes that open windows on other worlds than 'faery lands forlorn'.

The stresses in language are apparent not only in the presentation of character. Running through the novel is a vein of inflated diction and literary allusion which appears singularly inappropriate to a novel embodying working-class consciousness; it produces a self-conscious literariness which might be more appropriate to a modernist text. This commences with the first of several Shakespearian echoes, when Harry reflects on the absurdity of life whilst working in the pawnshop: 'So it would continue, week after week, a tale, told by an idiot, never to be concluded until the characters had no further use for pawning or redeeming anything else in this perplexing world.' This layer of literary allusion and its consequent inappropriateness become more strongly foregrounded later. The chapter in which Harry and Helen go for their seaside holiday on Harry's winnings is entitled 'Magic Casements': one of several references to Keats's *Ode to a Nightingale*.[11] The chapter headings themselves reveal a marked diversity of expression: 'Historical Narrative', 'No Vacancies', 'Magic Casements'. In the final chapter of Part Two of the novel, the romantic interlude bears scrutiny. The characters' attitudes to holidays link them to the illusory dream world which makes reality

[11]Op. cit., p. 65, 'opiaties'; p. 251, 'forlorn sense'; p. 150, 'heart ache'.

bearable: the anodyne sphere of betting, alcohol, cigarettes and advertisements into which most characters are drawn. The romantic language of the chapter is ambiguous: Helen's feelings about the holiday seem to be treated sincerely, if again in a linguistically inappropriate manner:

> To her all was of the quality of a sweet dream: too sweet; caused one to move about in a trance-like state of incredulity half the time. How different, ineffably different from the crude, vulgar warnings of the married women at the mill who had offended her ears by the references to the opportunities she and Harry would have for sexual indulgences.

At the same time, the language has a patently artificial quality, nearer to the 'opiates' of 'cheap novelettes or the spectacle of films' which Helen has previously tried to reject. The writing here is a cross between popular romantic fiction and D.H. Lawrence at his worst: 'the sounds would recede and a delicious indolence drug the brain', or: 'She lay back in the bracken, sighing. He brushed her sunburnt cheek with his lips. She murmured his name, her lips sought his, and, abandoning themselves, they surrendered to ecstatic oblivion.' If intended for a middle-class readership, the style also verges on parody, as though Harry and Helen themselves become one of the advertisements they had looked at together portraying a world to which they have no access. The contrast between expressions such as the 'silver ribbon' of the road in the holiday village and the 'mephitic black entries' of Hanky park is highlighted in a similar manner as the presentation of Sally's plight when she prostitutes herself to Sam Grundy after Larry Meath's death. Again the literary echoes of *Hamlet* and *Ode to a Nightingale* accentuate psychological and social conflict and contradiction by their incongruity: 'money that would give the quietus to gnawing memory', or watching her father and brother depart, 'Sally watched them go, torn between conflicting emotions, a fugitive response to their pleasure, then a blank, forlorn sense of utter loneliness which made her feel as one apart, a tresspasser, unable to share in that happiness of which she had been the cause.' Sally's alienation is conveyed in a language which is increasingly in conflict with the spoken words of Hanky Park's inhabitants: as she capitulates to the system of economic forces her construction as romantic and tragic heroine is heightened. The features of the language which express her point of view, its smooth, soporific rhetoric and literary allusiveness, compose an individual subject in keeping with a bourgeois literary tradition but whose linguistic homogeneity is under considerable strain in the context of the contradictory registers which the text foregrounds. The crucial question is whether the text colludes in this illusion and is thus blind to its ideology, or whether it highlights its own inconsistencies. I would suggest that the latter is the case, or at least that the novel can be re-read so that Greenwood's divided language is not a form of collusion but rather a reflection and revelation of the divisions in literary and social processes. It is in fact appropriate that the identity Sally acquires towards the end of the novel is only 'real' in conventional realist terms, thus emphasizing the falseness of the values she eventually accepts. It is as if Greenwood had anticipated a point made by Terry Eagleton commenting on Roland Barthes's essay *Writing Degree Zero*: 'There is no doubt that the "guilt" of which Barthes speaks is the guilt of the institution of Literature itself – an institution which, as he comments, testifies to the division of languages and the division of classes. To write in a "literary" way, in modern society, is inevitably to collude with such divisiveness.'[12]

Similar forms of tension are manifested in the 'Magic Casements' chapter. Language is foregrounded in Harry's thoughts: 'A glimmer of the significance of the word "beautiful" began to dawn on him . . . what was meant by its opposite "unbeautiful" struck him vividly. Hanky Park was "unbeautiful".' Such realizations of meaning and opposition lead Harry to reflect on the determinist nature of capitalism: 'Except that money would solve the problem; with this they could prolong their stay here as long as the money lasted.' Their escape is no escape. The vicious circles and oppositions of language and economic forces are condensed in the central image of the novel, the revolutions of automatic machinery. 'Then a rebuke rose to his mind by way of an afterthought; a disturbing picture of automatic and other devilishly self-sufficient machinery.' The individual, his love and his language are subsumed by anonymous and indifferent powers whose tentacles reach the seaside village. Indeed, such a holiday and such happiness are not illusory or elusive in the purely romantic, pseudo-metaphysical sense of Keats's 'magic casements' and nightingale, but rather in the specific ideological function that this kind of interlude and associated memories perform in the lives of the working class: Harry's parents and other characters have 'brief holidays by the seas that made the heart ache with their beauty'. It could be that the heart aches in fact not for the unique, isolated experience of happiness but because this relationship between pleasure and work forms part of a wider dialectical structure than the argument of Keats's ode does. The connection between betting – the possibility of acquiring fantastic wealth by chance or luck, also an activity with a significant ideological dimension – and the holiday assembles in the text a set of factitious relations which offer no solution to Harry, in fact they ultimately deny his sense of individuality and autonomy. The holiday creates an ironic circle, contrasting the obscure forces of capitalism with the individual subject's recognition of his inability to act independently which is an inversion of the design of the traditional realist novel. Helen has already given voice to the contradictions which Harry discovers as a consequence of unemployment, the oppositions of 'daft dreams' and 'harsh reality'. For Helen, 'All was a tangle; reality was too hideous to look upon: it could not be shrouded or titivated for long by the reading of cheap novelettes or the spectacle of films of spacious lives. They were only opiates and left a keener edge on hunger, made more loathsome reality's sores.'

The ideology of individualism is most conspicuous in the presentation of

[12]Terry Eagleton, *Literary Theory* (Oxford, Blackwell, 1983), p. 141.

Harry's character. His ingenuous ambitions of acquiring status and identity and his initial exhilaration when first engaged at Marlowe's are the illusions of his mis-recognition of himself and his relationship with the industrial environment: 'to be entrusted with a lathe; a machine. Machines! MACHINES! Lovely, beautiful word!' Machines, and more significantly the language of machinery, charm Harry into a romanticized and inflated view of himself.

> But he was in charge of a lathe at last even though it was of the simplified capstan variety. He regarded it with pride of possession, ran his hand along it caressingly, touched its mechanism and stared. . . . He felt vastly pleased with himself, more especially when he remembered that Tom Hare, who had served three months longer than he, had been put to a drilling machine.

Possession, fetishism and competition, and then a fight with Tom Hare and a temporary reconciliation with a cigarette: the factory floor is 'incarnadined' with more than the blood from Tom's nose. The machinery rapidly comes to signify a reversal of the situation as Harry initially perceived it. The machine takes possession of Harry, he becomes merely an appendage to the machine as Marx expressed it. A central or totalizing metaphor of circularity emerges; the lathe's revolutions become 'remorseless' as Harry stares at it and the full implications of language, machinery and work are brought home to him in Part Two of the novel. The 'awful indefiniteness' of the newspaper headlines replaces the thrill of a year ago when, 'the headline had seemed so full of promise of impending universal joy'. The machinery now reveals a different promise:

> Remember the installation of that new automatic machinery previous to the wholesale dismissal of Billy Higgs's generation? At that time it had held no significance for him except that it had meant promotion; it was merely newer and more up-to-date machinery whose functions were marvellous, whose capacity was manifold and infinite. The screw-cutting lathe that needed only the assistance of a hand to switch on the current; that could work ceaselessly, remorselessly, twenty-four hours a day, seven days a week without pause for meals; a Thing that fed itself, functioned with mathematical precision, 'could do anything except talk', as someone had put it.

The essential quality of the machinery is its cyclical movement which eliminates the human, the endlessly rotating circularity – reinforced in the above quotation by the syntactic parallelisms: a form of parataxis which dulls the reader's mind in turn – which becomes the pattern of life imposed on the inhabitants of Hanky Park. Harry is drawn into this vortex after two years at Marlowe's works.

Until now a year had seemed an interminable age, something that stretched away into the hazy infinity of the future and could not be comprehended. In a flash he saw twelve months each treading on the other's heel in a never-ending suffocating circle, monotonous, constrained, like prisoners exercising mechanically in the confines of the prison yard.

The image of imprisonment runs through the text along with that of circularity. The action, plot, narrative structure and characters' views work to subvert the conventional aspects of individualism, progression, linearity and resolution which compose the underlying teleology of a realist text's form. The cyclical pattern of life around the pawnshop is repeated on a smaller scale by Mrs Nattle's services to the community: when the transaction is completed the return is 'to some local hovel within whose walls were daily played the same scenes by the same cast with brain-dulling monotony'. Harry anticipates going through the same series of events as the previous generation of apprentices when he sees Billy Higgs unemployed and ragged, whereas Sally fails to appreciate that Mrs Dorbell and others were once young and in the same state as herself. Sally, 'feeling at a harsh discord with life', and seeing a vision of her future at the mill 'day in and day out, an eternal grind'; accompanied by 'the hideous noise of the shuttle's traverse', is driven to the only alternative – to prostitute herself to Sam Grundy. Her thoughts and actions and the tragic circle of life in Hanky Park are poignantly confirmed by her father's thoughts after striking her.

> *Did* he really wish her to live such a life as her mother had lived; such a life as was in store for young Harry and his wife? No! he answered himself emphatically, No! One long succession of dreary, monotonous years, toiling, moiling, with a pauper or near-pauper funeral at the end of it.

The most striking examples of circularity are in the climax of the action and the plot, and in the novel's closing scene. The final stages are mainly concerned with Harry's plight and the predicament of his sister Sally. Harry, having married the now pregnant Helen, has lost his job and been thrown out of his parents' home and is living desolately with Helen's parents. Tramping the streets looking for work and always being rejected, he degenerates physically and mentally. There seems to be no possibility of employment, and the full significance of his plight is brought home to him in the realization that he is a prisoner: 'The walls of the shops, houses and places of amusement were his prison walls; lacking money to buy his way into them the doors were all closed against him. That was the function of doors and walls; they were to keep out those who hadn't any money.' The situation becomes incongruously and ironically sharpened with inflated literary diction again, 'Where can a man go who hasn't any money? Wide, wide world; boundless firmament. He stood, wide-eyed, staring, palpitant, afraid.' The developing sense of contradiction in Harry's experience, and its presentation, has been anticipated in the posters which he notices at the labour exchange. Some of these promise a new life via emigration, depictions in which the unemployed exploited figure becomes in turn a prosperous exploiter of labour once established in Canada. There is also a bill giving warning of an unemployed man who had misrepresented his benefit claim and been sentenced to three months' hard labour. The cruel paradox or contradiction implies that work can be obtained through criminal acts, and that to work is to be a prisoner as much as it is to be out of work: in their apparent opposition the posters reveal the fundamental contradictions of the capitalist system. There is, as Harry discovers, 'no escape' from such a system. When his moral scruples stop him from stealing cigarettes, whilst his friends Tom Hare and Bill Simmons are eventually apprehended, Harry is relieved and by conventional bourgeois standards has received his reward in moral terms by having a clean conscience. However, the plot revolves in a fully ironic and cruel circle, for the next time Harry meets Tom and Bill it is to find that they have been employed on the city buses: 'Allus y've got to do is t'get y'self pinched and sent to quod, do y'time, an' when y'come out Probation Officer or Court Missionary does rest. It's th' on'y way t'get a job nowadays.' Yet the city bus office proclaims 'No Vacancies' outside. The implication is that crime pays, that society is criminal and indirectly recognizes this by giving jobs to offenders; the lie outside the office is part of the lie of society. The path to reward and the maintenance of the status quo are exposed in the plot: rather than naturalizing such values, the text reveals the process of naturalization at work. This process is repeated with Sally's surrender to another aspect of society. Sam Grundy is the main representative of capitalist values, and though the novel lacks any fuller depiction of the bourgeois classes the values and forces Grundy stands for are more significant than the individual character. He runs a small-scale bookmaker's operation in the back streets of Hanky Park, but has connections with the police and business interests of a dubious nature elsewhere which are hinted at. As a small-time operator he typifies the corruption of the system most clearly when he persuades Ned Narkey to join the police. Narkey personifies a kind of brutish ignorance, perhaps embryonic fascism. His antagonism to Larry Meath who is the representative of socialism, as well his jealousy over Sally, makes it clear where the forces of law and order stand and how they are composed. After Larry Meath's death and faced with the grinding vision of an imprisoned future, Sally's submission to Sam Grundy's overtures eventually brings about a redemption for Harry and his father: they too, like Tom and Bill, are to be given jobs on the city buses. This ironic twist in the plot's conclusion again openly reinforces and thus reveals the contradictions at the heart of society: crime is a necessary, essential condition for capitalism to operate smoothly and unquestioningly. This is further emphasized in the closing scene of the novel, a description almost identical to that at the beginning of the second chapter in Part One.

5.30 A.M.

A drizzle was falling.

Ned Narkey, on his beat, paused under the street lamp at the corner of North Street. Its staring beams lit the million globules of fine rain powdering his cape. A cat, sitting on the doorstep of Mr Hulkington's, the grocer's shop, blinked at Ned, rose, tail in air, and pushed its body against Ned's legs.

'Gaaa-cher bloody thing,' he muttered, and lifted it a couple of yards with his boot.

The circle is complete. The inexorable pattern and relentless turning goes on, though the previously anonymous figure of the law is now replaced with Ned Narkey. The connections in the relations of power come to a conclusion with the alliance of Ned Narkey and the law, and what can be seen as collusion or conspiracy in social relationships is significantly presented in the form of an individualized presentation of the law: what is most *real* is also what is most deceptive and *false*. It could be argued that in avoiding the conventions of an ending of illusory resolution the alternative offered is one of bad faith, substituting negation for bourgeois values and thus denying the possibility of change and maintaining the status quo. However, ideology must be unmasked before it can be changed.

The pattern is reinforced with images of enclosure, imprisonment and religion: the 'ghost-like' women going to the grocer's shop 'looked like fat cassocked monks with cowls down', a repetition of the same similes used earlier in the text to describe women going to work or to the pawnshop. The religious allusion serves to reveal more clearly the network of power relations, the concealed pattern of connections. It may well be that Greenwood's depiction of capitalism extends no further than the individuals and particular shops or factories of Hanky Park in the first instance, but this is the way in which they normally appear – the manner in which they are naturalized and operate. There are though in addition to the contradictions contained in the character of Mr Price the pawnshop owner, a Justice of the Peace and prominent churchgoer, suggestions of a network of power relations which determines events in the imagery associated with the pawnshop and beyond. Mr Price himself is described in corpse-like terms, his 'skeletonic fingers as they plunged into the heaped money of the cash drawer', and Mrs Dorbell's 'skeletonic yellow hand', descriptions which perhaps contain an allusion to Marx's view of capitalism as dead labour living off living labour. The money in the pawnshop is the cash-nexus of Hanky Park and the determining language of the social relations of its occupants. Historical inevitability is sometimes suggested through realistic descriptions, the 'irresistible current' of factory workers or the relentless turning of the lathes. In addition, the underlying forces in the hidden configuration of connections symbolized in the pawnbroker's sign become a kind of unholy trinity for capitalism to be visited by the 'cassocked monks'.

Sam Grundy, the gross street-corner bookmaker, Alderman Ezekiah Grumpole, the money-lender proprietor of the Good Samaritan Clothing Club. Price the pawnbroker, each an institution that had grown up out of the people's discontent. Sam Grundy promised sudden wealth as a prize, deeper poverty as a penalty; the other two, Grumpole and Price, represented temporary relief at the expense of a future of entanglement. A trinity, the outward visible sign of an inward spiritual discontent; safety valves through which the excess of impending change could escape, vitiate and dissipate itself.

Triangular images are repeated: Price and Jones's pawnshop stands 'at one point of a triangle; the other two points were occupied, respectively by a church and a palatial beerhouse, each large, commodious and convenient'. Sam Grundy sets up his betting stand in a back entry 'shaped like a triangle'; stretching out beyond this particular pattern lie images of wider, unfathomable 'networks' of railway lines; a tangle of material and human relationships as the title of the second chapter in Part Three indicates. The only arbiter in human relations, the anodyne of the 'open wound' of distress, is money – as both Harry and Sally come to acknowledge; money allows social conditions to be concealed or disguised, especially when expressed in the insulating form of Sam Grundy's car.

The integration of power structures is articulated through the pattern of connections in the action, plot and language. As we have seen, internal contradictions are revealed in the discourse and narrative technique. The various levels of discourse, from regional dialect to literary allusion or latinism such as 'termagant', produce a series of fractures which rupture the smooth flow of realist language. These are complemented by a constantly shifting narrative focus and technique from versions of interior monologue to third person omniscient, a form of mimetic and diegetic interplay which has been discussed recently in the context of nineteenth-century fiction.[13] This is further developed by rapid switches in point of view and scene.

This reading of *Love on the Dole* is at variance with recent discussions of the novel. It has been my concern to suggest that the text can be read so that it can be seen to reveal rather than deny contradiction. The apparent unities of classic realism and bourgeois values are subverted in the plot and structure. Further to this, the historical image of the 1930s which is produced by the novel is not only a passive reflection of working-class conditions in documentary realism: the contradictions and collusions inherent in capitalist social processes are unfolded through the tensions and patterns of language, image and plot. This reading then would argue

[13]David Lodge, '*Middlemarch* and the Idea of the Classic Realist Text', in Arnold Kettle, ed., *The Nineteenth Century Novel: Critical Essays and Documents* (London, Heinemann, 1981, 2nd edn); and Graham Martin, '*The Mill on the Floss* and the Unreliable Narrator', in Anne Smith, ed., *George Eliot: Centenary Essays and an Unpublished Fragment* (London, Vision Press, 1980).

that *Love on the Dole* declares its ideology – is aware of the contradictions in fiction – though set in a literary convention whose function is more often to obscure this area. In linking the conspiracy or plot of fiction to that of capitalist society perhaps a new aesthetic, not apparently free-standing but clearly linked to its ideological position, is possible for the novel.

Note

For details of the editions used in preparing this essay, see the footnotes.

Life

D.H. Lawrence was born in 1885 at Eastwood, Nottinghamshire, the son of a collier. A talented child, he won a scholarship to Nottingham High School, eventually becoming a pupil-teacher in his home village, and then proceeding to Nottingham University for his teacher's diploma. He published his first short stories in *The English Review*, and some poetry. His first novel, *The White Peacock*, which he had been working on for over five years, appeared in 1911. His next important novel, based on his own and his family's lives, was *Sons and Lovers* (1913). By this time he had given up school-teaching and for the remainder of his life earned his living by writing. In 1914 he married Mrs Frieda Weekley (née von Richthofen) with whom he had left England in 1912, and whose influence on his work was considerable. Other important novels are *The Rainbow* (1915), *Women in Love* (1917), *Kangaroo* (1923), *The Plumed Serpent* (1926), and *Lady Chatterley's Lover* (1928). Poems, short and long stories also poured from Lawrence's pen, and a considerable body of literary and social criticism, easily available in *A Selection from Phoenix*, ed. A.P.H. Inglis (London, Penguin, 1968) and *Selected Literary Criticism*, ed. Antony Beal (London, Heinemann, 1955). In 1919, Lawrence and his wife left England, and stayed for periods in Italy, Sicily, Australia, New Mexico and Mexico, finally returning to Europe in 1923. Lawrence's last visit to England took place in 1926. He spent his final years near Florence, but the tuberculosis that had long afflicted him required a move to Vence, near Nice, where he died in 1930. The standard biography is by Harry T. Moore, *The Priest of Love* (London, Heinemann, 1974) which prints in an appendix a full list of his published books.

Criticism

There is a very large accumulation of secondary writing about Lawrence. The title under his name in the Fontana Modern Masters series (London, 1972), by Frank Kermode, may be recommended both for itself and for its useful Select Bibliography. Graham Hough, *The Dark Sun* (London, Duckworth, 1958) offers a helpful survey. F.R. Leavis, *D.H. Lawrence: Novelist* (London, Chatto & Windus, 1955), the book which more than any other established Lawrence's modern reputation, is worth consulting though now may be thought too polemically engaged. An interesting recent work is Graham Holderness *D.H. Lawrence: History, Ideology and Fiction* (Dublin, Gill and Macmillan, 1982). Cambridge University Press are currently bringing out a fresh edition of his works, with reliable texts. Lawrence's social thinking is surveyed in Raymond Williams, *Culture and Society, 1780–1950*, part II, chapter 2 (London, Chatto & Windus, 1958). For a discussion of 'class' in Lawrence's novels, see the essay by the present writer in *The Uses of Fiction: Essays on the Modern Novel in Honour of Arnold Kettle* (Milton Keynes, Open Univ. Press, 1982), edited by Douglas Jefferson and Graham Martin. A good selection of essays is *D.H. Lawrence: A Critical Survey* (London, Forum House, 1969), edited by Harry T. Moore. The latter's two-volume edition of Lawrence's *Collected Letters* (London, Heinemann, 1962) provides much critical insight into his work.

5

'History' and 'Myth' in D.H. Lawrence's Chatterley Novels

Graham Martin

Lawrence's last prose work was *Apocalypse*. Written towards the end of 1929 and originally intended as an introduction to Frederick Carter's *The Dragon of the Apocalypse*, it was set aside unfinished, to be posthumously published in 1931. It ends with these words:

> What we want is to destroy our false, inorganic connections, especially those related to money, and re-establish the living organic connections, with the cosmos, with the sun and earth, with mankind and nation and family. Start with the sun, and the rest will slowly, slowly, happen.[1]

Frank Kermode has proposed that *Apocalypse* is the key metaphysical work of Lawrence's final period, with a close and immediate relevance to *Lady Chatterley's Lover*.[2] Connie's story represents her initiation into the mysteries of the phallic consciousness (a concept more complex and radical in Lawrence's thinking than 'sexual'), whereby the 'living organic connections with the cosmos' are restored and being 'alive in the flesh'[3] becomes life's great and central wonder. The England of the 1920s set before us by the novel is enduring the deathly pre-apocalyptic Last Days, begun in the 1914–18 war, and extending into the immediate future, that 'bad time coming . . . [of] death and destruction, for these industrial masses' prophesied in Mellors' letter to Connie at the end of the novel.[4] Only mystical rebirth into the old pagan consciousness can rescue the English from the strangling obsession of money-lust, from 'mentalism', from fixated and mechanical social forms. Wragby and its traditions, the literary world where Clifford strives for reputation, the industrial projects he takes up, the social *milieu* of Connie's father glimpsed in the Riviera episode, the semi-urbanized world of the mining villages that surround Wragby, all these are evidence of the living death of the Last Days. Connie and Mellors

[1]D.H. Lawrence, *Apocalypse, And the Writings on Revelation*, ed. Mara Kalnins (Cambridge, Cambridge UP, 1980), p. 149.
[2]Frank Kermode, *Lawrence* (London, Fontana/Collins, 1973), pp. 119–32.
[3]Lawrence, *Apocalypse*, p. 149.
[4]D.H. Lawrence, *Lady Chatterley's Lover* (London, Penguin, 1960), p. 315.

alone achieve that difficult exemplary rebirth which must precede the new life affirmed in Mellors' letter, and symbolized in Connie's coming child.

Kermode (as he says) bases his argument on the third Chatterley novel, privately printed in Florence in 1928, but (pirated copies apart) not publicly available before the Heinemann edition of 1960. This novel was preceded by two earlier works, one printed as *The First Lady Chatterley* (New York, Dial Press, 1944; London, Heinemann, 1972), the second as *John Thomas and Lady Jane* (London, Heinemann, 1972). Lawrence began the first in October 1926, wrote the second presumably during 1927, and the third in the winter of 1927–8.[5] I propose to argue here that whatever the place of apocalyptic thinking in the genesis and writing of the novels, they were also prompted by Lawrence's last visit to the Eastwood area in mid September 1926.[6] In one respect, this proposal may seem obvious to the point of banality. The 'spirit of place' was usually a factor in the genesis of Lawrence's writings. It is well known that the setting of the Chatterley novels is 'the country of [his] heart',[7] as he described this in an often-quoted letter written after he had returned from England to Florence, where all three novels were drafted. The fictional Wragby and Tevershall, the contrast between the gamekeeper's woodland home, with the industrial environment which threatens it, Connie's forays into Uthwaite, the earlier life of Mrs Bolton, are directly based on the Eastwood district. There is also, mainly in the first two novels, a scatter of real place-names: Nottingham, Sheffield, Hardwick Hall; Hucknall, Annesley, Underwood and Heanor, villages near Eastwood; even Felley Mill and Haggs Farm. This is the region which Lawrence calls in the same letter 'real England – the hard pith of England',[8] and the Chatterley novels represent his last hymn, albeit a despairing hymn, to it. Yet there is a more particular reason than 'the spirit of place' for proposing Lawrence's visit of September 1926 as a formative influence on the novels. Lawrence then saw with his own eyes direct evidence of the General Strike, still sustained by the mineworkers. This too he mentions in his letter ('they've pushed a spear through the side of *my* England'[9]), and it is the source and occasion of the political and social emphasis of the novels, especially of the first two. If we think of this as 'history', and the apocalyptic dimension noted by Kermode as 'myth', then evidently in the third novel, 'history' has been substantially displaced by 'myth', and being the best known of the three, it has come to stand for Lawrence's final statement. But only by considering all three novels can we grasp the measure of that displacement from 'history' to 'myth'. *The First Lady Chatterley* and *John Thomas and Lady Jane*, though sharing common ground with *Lady Chatterley's Lover* are not

[5]Harry T. Moore, *The Priest of Love* (London, Heinemann, 1974), pp. 422–3; *The Collected Letters of D.H. Lawrence*, ed. Harry T. Moore (London, Heinemann, 1962) II, pp. 944, 970, 1026, 1033.
[6]Moore, *The Priest of Love*, p. 421.
[7]*Collected Letters* II, pp. 951–2.
[8]*Op. cit.*, p. 953.
[9]*Op. cit.*, p. 952.

earlier versions of it; they are in themselves, distinct novels. Alternatively, we might think of all three novels as a single composite text, registering Lawrence's evolving response to the 'history' glimpsed during his visit to the English Midlands in September 1926, a response characterized by two contradictory impulses: to engage with the 'history', and to withdraw from it. The balance between engagement and withdrawal changes from novel to novel, but a struggle between them equally marks all three.

Lawrence's rendering of the 'history' may be approached by way of a little-known essay, 'Return to Bestwood',[10] recounting his impressions of the Strike, gained while he stayed a few days as his sister's at Ripley, some six miles from their old Eastwood home. The essay registers a more complex and divided state of mind than is represented by the sentence 'I hate the damned place', which his biographer quotes as Lawrence's last verdict on Eastwood.[11] The signs of the Strike are detailed with a mixture of feelings: mild outrage at the sight of women in the Eastwood marketplace, where his mother used to shop (*vide Sons and Lovers*, chapter 4), barracking police-men appointed to guard blacklegs on their way home and defiantly waving red flags; disengaged observant sympathy for the out-of-work colliers everywhere to be seen 'slowly loafing, fishing, poaching in spite of all notices . . . [or] squatted on their heels, on the wayside, silent and watch-ful';[12] hostile wonder that the police are not English, but from Ireland or Scotland, unlike the old days of friendly local bobbies; touches of acute insight into the three-way silent and watchful antagonism between striking colliers, blacklegs coming off shift, and protective police guard, and an overall nostalgia for the miners as they used to be, vigorous, gay, fierce, potentially wild, in contrast with the passive, innerly-despairing figures he now sees. Nothing is said about the issues of the Strike, of the hopes and affirmations which preceded it. The sense of imminent defeat is powerfully conveyed, and equally that the whole event is portentous; but the cause is said to lie, not in the immediate political and economic struggle of which the Strike was the culmination, but in a psychological change in the miners themselves. Lawrence dates this change after the war. 'Till 1920 there was a strange power of life in them, something wild and urgent, that one could hear in their voices.'[13] But now they are silent, ghostly. Though men of his own generation, he now feels a stranger amongst them. The tone of his account to this point is that of a 'revenant' to a once-loved world, now unaccountably deteriorated, as if to say: 'this is no longer my place, nor its evident crisis my concern.' Yet it is here that the essay reverses direction. Lawrence declares that the miners are 'the only people who move me strongly'. Men like himself, they are 'in the life sense of the word, good'.

[10]First printed in D.H. Lawrence, *Phoenix II*, ed. Warren Roberts and Harry T. Moore (London, Heinemann, 1968). The text is reprinted in D.H. Lawrence, *A Selection from Phoenix*, ed. A.P.H. Inglis (London, Penguin, 1971), pp. 146–57. Page references here are to this text.

[11]Moore, *The Priest of Love*, p. 421.

[12]Lawrence, *A Selection from Phoenix*, p. 153.

[13]*Op. cit.*, p. 154.

He then lists, as it were in opposition to the terms over which he believed the Strike was being fought, ideas which deserve more prominence in writing about Lawrence.

> I know that we could, if we would, establish little by little a true democracy in England: we could nationalize the land and industries and means of transport, and make the whole thing work infinitely better than at present, *if we would*. It all depends on the spirit in which the thing is done.
>
> I know we are on the brink of a class war. I know that we had all better hang ourselves at once, than enter on a struggle that shall be a fight for the ownership or non-ownership of property, pure and simple, and nothing beyond. I know the ownership of property is a problem that may have to be fought out. But beyond the fight must lie a new hope, a new beginning. . . .
>
> I know we must take up responsibility for the future, now. A great change is coming, and must come. What we need is some glimmer of vision of a world that shall be, beyond the change.
>
> . . . What we should live for is life and the beauty of aliveness, imagination, awareness, contact. To be perfectly alive is to be immortal.[14]

'Return to Bestwood' can be thought of as the first notes for the Chatterley novels. Details like a car-drive through the district are the seed of key passages in the novels. The date 1920, selected for the change in the miners' attitude to life, provides the starting point for the action of the story, when the Chatterleys return to Wragby. The climate of incipient industrial unrest, of the miners' class feeling about mine-owner families like the Chatterleys, has its roots in Lawrence's observations. But above all, the combination of contradictory feelings towards the mining communities, of despairing rejection, of continuing commitment, though commitment on very Lawrentian terms, which the essay so strikingly shows, dominates all three novels. As he remarks elsewhere, 'tragedy ought really to be a great kick at misery'.[15] 'Return to Bestwood' is notable for registering the fact of a social tragedy, and for kicking against it. As such, it makes a valuable *prolegomenon* to the three Chatterley novels.

On 31 October 1926, Frieda Lawrence wrote to her son from the Villa Mirende, Florence, whither she and Lawrence had returned from their visit to England:

> Lawrence goes into the woods to write, he is writing a short long story, always breaking new ground, the curious class feeling this time or

[14]*Op. cit.*, pp. 156–7.
[15]*Collected Letters* I, p. 150.

rather the soul against the body, no I don't explain it well, the *animal* part.[16]

The theme of 'the animal part' in the Chatterley novels is sufficiently familiar, that of 'the curious class feeling' less so. Yet in the first two novels, it is central, and its relatively smaller role in the third an evident case of the displacement from 'history' to 'myth'. We can see this most easily in the contrast between Oliver Mellors, and his analogues in the previous novels. Mellors, it will be recalled, though of working-class origin, appears in the novel as effectively de-classed. As a boy, he was clever and 'literary', attending Sheffield Grammar School. His first job was as a clerk in the offices of a mining firm. He experienced a long painful 'cultured' friendship with a school-teacher's daughter, passionate in its own way, but excluding sex. From this, he turned to the 'common' and sensual Bertha Coutts,[17] to manual work as a blacksmith, exchanging the 'proper English' he'd learned at school for the local dialect. Then came the war. Mellors joined a cavalry regiment, was promoted lieutenant, and formed a close friendship with his colonel. As the Chatterley gamekeeper, he is thus a social misfit, a point noted by Clifford, and by Connie, who thinks him at their first meeting in manner and speech 'almost a gentleman'.[18] Socially, he is at ease with Connie's father, intellectually he is Connie's equal. He now has a command of both educated English and the dialect, and alternates between them with deliberation. Mellors thus emerges from this complicated personal history a self-divided man, keenly aware of being an outsider, and it is mainly through his exacerbated consciousness that Lawrence, in conversations between Mellors and Connie, sets out 'the condition of England' as it is envisaged in the novel. On the issue of class, Mellors is disgusted with every aspect of it – with 'the curious rubber-necked toughness and unlivingness of the middle and upper classes' (instanced in some degree by Clifford's set), and with the 'pettiness' and 'vulgarity of manner' of his own class, above all with its obsession with money. Conceding that the poor *had* to care about money, he yet insists that such care was 'like a great cancer, eating away the individuals of all classes. He refused to *care* about money'.[19] In a moment of faint social hope, he wonders whether bosses and colliers might be weaned away from working merely for money, towards a commitment to beauty, life, awareness, those familiar Lawrentian values. Yet nothing of this kind is attempted. His deeper conviction is one of nihilistic despair. 'Bolshevism' he sees as yet another manifestation of the obsessed materialism of the industrial age, and in its destructive energies, portent of the coming catastrophe, 'the extermination of the human species'.[20] We may say that

[16]*Op. cit* II, p. 944.
[17]*Lady Chatterley's Lover*, p. 210. This, and all subsequent page references to the three Chatterley novels are to the Penguin editions.
[18]*Op. cit.*, p. 48.
[19]*Op. cit.*, pp. 147–8.
[20]*Op. cit.*, p. 227.

Mellors can carry this burden of denunciation and prophecy precisely because he has *been* declassed. In this respect, the novel changes him not at all. It merely confirms that thorough-going alienation from both the working and the owning classes, which is his condition when we first meet him. Correspondingly, Connie's discovery of phallic consciousness in her relation with Mellors goes hand-in-hand with an alienation from her class. The narrative of the 'myth', it may be added, requires nothing less from each of them.

The gamekeeper in the earlier novels, Oliver Parkin by name, is both a simpler figure, and more emphatically working-class. Between *The First Lady Chatterley* and *John Thomas and Lady Jane* there are significant differences of presentation, but the shared contrasts with the third novel are worth noting. In each earlier case, Parkin, though personally solitary and at enmity with the colliers who poach the Chatterley woods, belongs still amongst his own people. Neither is, in Mellors' style, educated, intellectual; there is no meeting in a London club with Connie's father, man to man. In the relationship with Connie, 'class' is an issue, Connie being suspected, not unjustly, of social patronage, and how two such different people might make a common life is seen as a genuine, if not insuperable, bar to their marriage. Parkin's class situation, first as a working-man dependent on Clifford's yea-or-nay, then after leaving the Chatterley estate, as a labourer on a weekly wage in a Sheffield steel mill, is entirely explicit. Each earlier novel, unlike the third, contains a scene when Connie visits the working-class Tewson family in a Sheffield working-class house and street, where Parkin is lodging. Here, she sees Parkin no longer the glamorous lover of the Chatterley woods, but as a mere working-man, with strained shoulder and hands calloused from the unaccustomed heavy labour in the mill. Connie also shares in a family high tea round a crowded living-room table, of ham, tongue, tinned peaches and pears, plum cake, tarts, and the best china on show. The scene is of further intrinsic interest, as the occasion when Bill Tewson, who got Parkin his job in the steel mill, discusses earnestly with Connie the relationship between the classes, Clifford's and his own. 'Realism' is a term that recent criticism has made controversial, but it may fairly be applied to categorize such differences between the first two novels and the later, in the presentation of the gamekeeper. Parkin is conceived as a figure neither wholly unrepresentative of his class, nor in radical opposition to it; whereas Mellors in both these ways is the atypical product of a specific personal history, enabling him to become the vehicle for a recognizably Lawrentian jeremiad.

Some differences between the two Parkins can now be considered. Towards the conclusion of *The First Lady Chatterley*, the gamekeeper expresses both class loyalty and a political commitment as determining factors in his future life, with or without Connie. In scenes with no equivalent in the later novels (following Parkin's move to Sheffield and Connie's visit to the Tewsons) the lovers meet by chance in Tevershall. Together with Connie's intellectual friend, Duncan Forbes, they drive to Southwell, where Connie and Parkin debate their future. She proposes that they buy a

farm with her money, which he will work. He refuses on the grounds of
losing his independence, and of loyalty to those like Bill Tewson who have
no such easy option. She cannot understand this, accusing him of small-
mindedness about money. They quarrel, explicitly on the grounds that on
her terms he would not be master in his own house, which he determines to
be. And on this note of deadlock, they part. But in a later conversation
with Forbes, different reasons for Parkin's obduracy emerge, not known to
Connie. He is the secretary of the Communist League at the Sheffield
works. 'It's something as I've laid hold of, an' I can't let go – like an
electric thing. Ay, it's a sure thing.' Forbes, sympathetic to such ideas,
advises him to plan on marrying Connie, stick to his job and live near Sheffield, and this Parkin decides to do. Forbes discovers in Parkin at this point:

> a glow of soft human power, which made Duncan suddenly see demo-
> cracy in a new light, men kindled to this glow of human beauty and
> awareness, opened glowing to another sort of contact.[21]

Such sentences, in this context, show Lawrence giving tentative political
form to the abstract hopes for the future listed in 'Return to Bestwood'.
Throughout the novel, Parkin's class antagonism is marked, but only after
he turns from his life as a solitary gamekeeper to that of an ordinary
working-man does this take a political direction. During the discussion
with Connie at the Tewson's, the question Bill hopes Connie will answer is:
do the gentry like Clifford have the same feelings as men like himself? or
do power and riches make a final difference? Conceding a good deal to this
charge, she claims nevertheless that 'there are some quite human people
even among the upper classes'. It is Parkin who insists on an absolute
distinction:

> The working-class is devils, and the upper class is another sort of devils.
> But in the working-class you come to an end of their devilment. An' wi'
> th' upper class, you canna. They've always got a door shut in your face,
> an' they're always behind the door, laughing at you.[22]

What the upper classes finally deny is 'contact', ultimate relationship with
other men. Partly this is a thrust at Connie, but it summarizes Connie's
own view of Clifford's class. The novel ends with her utter rejection of
Wragby and all it stands for because of 'the life-contact'[23] she had achieved
with Parkin, symbolized in their coming child. Her view of Parkin's political ideas remains ambiguous, but the reiteration of the term 'contact' certainly invites us to imagine a potential sympathy. The novel, then, leaves
us with a promise, not confined simply to their personal relationship. Or
rather, in the characterization of Parkin, it provides for that relationship a

[21] *The First Lady Chatterley* (London, Penguin, 1973), p. 219.
[22] *Op. cit.*, p. 178.
[23] *Op. cit.*, p. 228.

not unhopeful public dimension, an engagement with 'history'.

In *John Thomas and Lady Jane*, Parkin is no less possessed of antagonism towards the upper classes, symbolized in his employer Clifford, but the political dimension has entirely disappeared. In the discussion at the Tewson's it is Bill who is the convinced socialist, pressing Connie about whether the upper class feel any guilt about their monopoly of the good things of life, or sense that they might share it with other classes. He even puts the socialist critique of bourgeois nationalism.

> They say as our rich people feels much more kindred feeling with other rich people, whether they're Americans or Germans or Russians or Jews or anything, then they do with us, their own countrymen. It isn't *Germans* they're holding out against, and afraid of: it's us working-men, who are Englishmen the same as they are an' in a big majority when it comes to.[24]

But Parkin takes little part in the conversation, dismissing it as all talk which gets nowhere. Socialism offers no hope. For him, everybody is alike in their desire for money. The vision of incipient democracy glimpsed in the Parkin of *The First Lady Chatterley* finds no expression in this second characterization. He feels no real link with Tewson, and looks for no future at the steel mill. Living in the Tewson house stifles him, and he decides to leave as soon as possible, to find work locally as a farm-labourer. Such promise as the conclusion offers remains at the personal level: that he and Connie may, somehow, make a life together on whatever terms seem possible, even going to live in Italy. Earlier in the novel, in contrast with *The First Lady Chatterley*, Connie is said to realize that

> Class is an anachronism. It finished in 1914. Nothing remains but a vast proletariat, including kings, aristocrats, squires, millionaires and working people, men and women alike. And then a few individuals who had not been proletarianized![25]

These few individuals were 'the warm-blooded' like Parkin and herself, 'the cold-blooded' being the condition of the proletariat. The social and economic definition of class which in the first novel coexists with Parkin's definition quoted above is replaced in *John Thomas and Lady Jane* by this entirely psychological definition. Though defined within his own class, and as little intellectual as his predecessor, the second Parkin is gradually abstracted from it. His fate, moreover, is interpreted within a structure of ideas (of which the above paragraph is an example) provided discursively by the *narrator*. Thus, despite his personal qualities of fierce and tenacious independence, he is more passively conceived, lacking the political commitment of the first Parkin, as well as the prophetic quality of his successor

[24] *John Thomas and Lady Jane* (London, Penguin, 1973), p. 365.
[25] *Op. cit.*, p. 294.

Mellors. Where the latter chooses his exile, and the first Parkin stays put, the second seems forced into flight.

Moreover, it is in *John Thomas and Lady Jane* that the element of 'myth' first appears. We have seen that Mellors is a divided character, in one sense a product of class, in another an outsider, an initiate of the phallic consciousness. Signs of this division appear in the first Parkin, but they are present only to Connie. When she first sees the gamekeeper washing himself outside his hut in the Chatterley woods, she has a vision of him as a body, separate and superior to the clothed socially-defined man. So, too, his passion for her emerges from some depth in him distinct from his social personality, and when Connie speaks of this he is incredulous. In *John Thomas and Lady Jane* this aspect of Parkin is very greatly developed.

We are told that in their night together at Parkin's hut, he introduces Connie to phallic, as distinct from merely sexual, consciousness, to 'the mysterious phallic godhead',[26] and when Connie tries to explain to her sister, that her relationship with Parkin will survive the problems of the social *mésalliance*, this becomes her argument (see chapter 14). As with the new account of class, these interpretations are, as it were, attached to the character and behaviour of Parkin, by narratorial comment, or in Connie's own thinking. Parkin himself, unlike Mellors, is not yet their explicit source. If in one respect *John Thomas and Lady Jane* should be seen with *The First Lady Chatterley*, in contrast with the third novel, in another it shows Lawrence elaborating round the simpler contours of the first novel, the ideas which will only find full *narrative* form by way of the character of Mellors.

These changes in the presentation of the gamekeeper thus show a disengagement from his class origins and milieu, and a resolution of his relationship with Connie which shifts from a possible location within the social and political world of the novel, through a personal flight from it, to its emphatic and principled rejection in a spirit of prophetic despair.

Yet if 'myth' begins to predominate in the second novel it is also true that 'history' remains distinctively present, in ways less directly connected with, but counter-balancing the changes in, the characterization of the gamekeeper. Two episodes may be cited. At the Wragby Christmas house-party, towards the beginning of the novel, Tommy Dukes, a character who makes no appearance in *The First Lady Chatterley*, is made spokesman for utopian possibilities implied in 'Return to Bestwood'. The conversation takes a political turn, prompted by references to the Russian Revolution, the possibility of one in England, and Wellsian ideas for a thoroughly mechanized future, where some women will be maintained for breeding purposes, others immunized and directed to other useful tasks. Connie intervenes:

> I can imagine a world where nobody cared terribly about money, or owning things, or bossing other people. Personally, I wouldn't care a bit

26*Op. cit.*, p. 239.

if the land and the mines and all those things belonged to everybody. I only want to live . . . where one needn't be desperate about owning anything. Where a bit of life flowed.

This is a version of Lawrence's non-possessive socialism, where ownership is less important than 'the flow of life'. Tommy Dukes responds:

There will be a civilization based on the mystery of touch, and all that means; a field of consciousness which hasn't yet opened into existence. . . . Oh, there'll be a democracy – the democracy of touch. For the few who surivive the fear of it. . . . We're only an experiment in mechanization, that will be properly used in the next phase.[27]

The prognostication concerns not only a far distant future but an element in Connie's relationship with Parkin. 'Life' can be reached by 'touch', as distinct from the assertion of the 'will', which creates the world of Clifford and the cold greedy industrial machine (*vide* pp. 111–15). Connie and Parkin achieve this relationship of 'touch', perhaps in itself a familiar enough Lawrentian theme. What is unusual is the political connotation supplied by Duke's phrase 'the *democracy* of touch'. Here one can see Lawrence attempting to appropriate for his own social thinking an idea which he usually connects with the degenerated mechanized modern world. In the third novel, we hear nothing of this 'democracy of touch'. Dukes is now a cheerfully brusque character, who speaks for some Lawrentian ideas ('one has to be human and have a heart and a penis if one is going to escape being either a god or a Bolshevist' – Bolshevism being another species of mechanism[28]), but in a merely 'mental' way. The further hope glimpsed by his predecessor finds no root in his mind.

The second episode is of weightier effect. It opens a long historical perspective on the action by means of a narratorial contribution to the account of Connie's car drive through Tevershall, the surrounding countryside, and to Uthwaite (the novel's fictional name for Chesterfield). This car journey is a feature of *The First Lady Chatterley* (chapter 6), and in less developed form, so is the historical perspective. But Lawrence elaborates greatly in the second novel, and in terms that survive into the third. Connie has viewed the ugly mining village of Tevershall with despair, and pondered Parkin's relationship with it. She drives on towards the new, postwar, thoroughly-mechanized colliery, Stacks Gate, whose profits had 'put hundreds of thousands of pounds into the Duke's pocket',[29] owner of Warsop Castle to be seen in the distance. She passes Cheswick (i.e. Hardwick) Hall, for all its noble Elizabethan proportions a mere monument to a dead past. She arrives in Uthwaite, an old market-town

[27]*Op. cit.*, pp. 64–5.
[28]*Lady Chatterley's Lover*, p. 41.
[29]*John Thomas and Lady Jane*, p. 157.

enveloped in the productions of the industrial age, railway lines, foundries, lorry traffic, and miners' dwellings, old and new, lining all the roads leading to and from it. Here Lawrence interpolates his own interpretation of what Connie has been seeing.

> They talked about England, but this is the heart of England. One meaning blots out another. The great houses, 'stately homes of England', still loom and make good photographs. But they are dead. . . . This is England. One meaning blots out another. So the mines were blotting out the halls. It was inevitable. When the great land-owners started the mines, and made new fortunes, they started also their own obliteration from the English countryside. One meaning blots out another.[30]

It may be noted in passing that no other English novel of its time presents so clearly as this paragraph within its context the character of the historical change coming about, the connection between the ownership of the land, the capitalization of the large mining concerns, the related industrialization of town and countryside, and the reflexive consequences for the owners and the houses which symbolized their ownership. (Leavis, it will be recalled, in one of his less fortunate judgements, praised *The Rainbow* for its record of 'essential social history';[31] he would have done better to keep the term for this aspect of *Lady Chatterley's Lover*.) In the novel as a whole, such analysis necessarily provides the novel's human events with a possible future, dialectically related to an observable present and a remembered past, running counter to the ahistoric implications of the 'myth'. Connie proceeds to envisage this future, both in hope and fear.

> The future! The far future! Out of the orgy of ugliness and of dismalness and of dreariness, would there, could there ever unfold a flower, a life with beauty in it? as a pure antithesis to what they had now. Could the descendants of these colliers ever make life a new and rather gorgeous thing? Could they? In the far future? After all this that existed at present was gone, smashed and abandoned, repudiated for ever – could the children of the miners make a new world, with mystery and sumptuousness in it? Her own children's children, if she had a child to Parkin? She shuddered a little, at the awful necessity for transition.[32]

Notice that she does not reject the transition, and she goes on to reflect that whereas now the miners and steelworkers were the victim-creatures of coal and iron, the time would come when *they* would dominate, when they would *use* the raw material of their labour 'for the flowering of their own bodies and anima, instead of as now, being used by it.'[33] If it can fairly be

[30]*Op. cit.*, p. 159.
[31]F.R. Leavis, *D.H. Lawrence: Novelist* (London, Chatto & Windus, 1955), p. 107.
[32]*John Thomas and Lady Jane*, pp. 162–3.
[33]*Op. cit.*, p. 164.

alleged of Lawrence's social ideas that they are usually 'idealist', disconnected from possible conceptions of ownership and productive work, such criticism cannot easily be applied to the above passage. We have seen that later in the novel, Parkin finds no final connection within himself with his class in its present state. Here, Connie sees the deepest possible connection between them, identifying 'the weird passion that was in Parkin'[34] with the forces that were transforming the visible world about her, while her own connection is established through him, and their child.

'Myth' dominates in the third novel, yet 'history' as registered in the account of Connie's car journey continues to haunt the story. The comparable passages (pp. 163–6) concentrate more on Connie's horror of the future, the notion of distant positive transformation disappears, yet the sense of underground energy and power (albeit in unhuman forms – 'men not men, but animas of coal and iron and clay')[35] remains. Mellors too, she recalls, is a child of these people, though with the significant qualification that things had gone much further since he was born. If in the second novel, 'history' sets up implications which cut against those of the incipient 'myth', so that the story is disturbed by opposing currents, in the third, 'myth' attempts to overcome 'history', to accommodate its perspective to the 'mythic' closure articulated in Mellors' final prophecy. Yet, even here, that element of 'realism' which few novels finally shake off maintains its challenge. We have seen that Mellors disengages as thoroughly as possible from the living death of England. Yet, still, he envisages a human future with Connie and the baby. And with Connie's income to sustain them, their disengagement from 'class' can hardly be thought complete.

Of one set of changes, those affecting the presentation of Clifford Chatterley, and friends, I have said nothing though they, too, offer revealing material for analysis as Lawrence changes the target of his attack from Platonism, to aestheticism, to spurious literary ambition and success. But underlying each example, the principal charges against Clifford are that he combines egoistic cold-heartedness with a rapacious will to dominate – whether Connie, or Mrs Bolton, or associates in his various schemes. He embodies those class characteristics responsible for the dreary mechanized industrialization of England and of its working people to set over against which there are only the values variously asserted by Parkin/Mellors and Connie. That theme changes in essence not at all, and few would care to contest its relevance to the 'history' which the different novels differently confront.

[34]*Op. cit.*, p. 161.
[35]*Lady Chatterley's Lover*, p. 166.

Note

Jack Common: Publications

The Freedom of the Streets (London, Secker and Warburg, 1938).
Seven Shifts, ed. with introduction by Common (London, Secker and Warburg, 1938; republished, Wakefield, E.P. Publishing, 1978).
Kiddar's Luck (London, Turnstile Press, 1951; Bath, Cedric Chivers, 1971; Glasgow, Blackie, 1974).
The Ampersand (London, Turnstile Press, 1954).
Kiddar's Luck and The Ampersand (Newcastle upon Tyne, Frank Graham, 1975).
Revolt Against An Age of Plenty, eds. Huw Beynon and Colin Hutchinson (Newcastle upon Tyne, Strong Words, 1980).
'Orwell at Wallington', *Stand* 22, 3 (1981), pp. 32–6.

The Jack Common Collection

The unpublished work of Jack Common – various short stories and the drafts of several novels – is housed in Newcastle University Library, and along with the rest of his papers (including many diaries and notebooks written in an often indecipherable script), these were painstakingly catalogued by Eileen Aird in January 1976. We are grateful to the University of Newcastle for permission to consult this material and to Jack Common's daughter, Mrs Sally Magill, for her kind agreement to its use in this essay.

Note: In the following essay we shall refer to the 1975 Frank Graham amalgamated edition of *Kiddar's Luck* and *The Ampersand*.

6

'A Revolutionary Materialist with a Leg Free': The Autobiographical Novels of Jack Common

Michael Pickering and Kevin Robins

> Might we not say that every child at play behaves like a creative writer, in that he creates a world of his own, or, rather, re-arranges the things of his world in a way which pleases him?
>
> Freud

Few people who have visited Marx's grave in Highgate Cemetery could have realized that part of the gigantic bust on top of the great man's tomb was modelled on a relatively unknown working-class writer from Newcastle upon Tyne. As the sculptor, Lawrence Bradshaw, explained: 'I decided to base Karl Marx's eyebrows on the fundamental structure of Jack Common's brow for here I found many of the human qualities that I could see in the photographs and I understood from reading the life of Karl Marx. Human sympathy, tolerance and a profound understanding and an inexhaustible patience. For Jack had tremendous patience with both his friends and with his own life.'[1] The anonymous afterlife which this unusual tribute bestows upon Common is a wry and fitting compliment. But who exactly was this neglected writer, this Geordie working man who was once described by his friend George Orwell as 'potentially a sort of Chesterton of the Left'?[2]

Born in 1903, the son of a Newcastle railwayman, he left school at the age of 14 and attended a course at a commercial college. This he found 'a sad swindle'. On leaving here, he secured a clerical post with a very old-fashioned firm of solicitors, and as he put it in his diary, 'expecting to come into a shining world of efficient money-making . . . I found myself a minor character in a Dickens story.'[3] This experience of college and solicitor's office, as well as of his childhood and youth in working-class Heaton, later served as the basic material for his own story, as told in his two autobiographical novels written in the 1950s: *Kiddar's Luck* and *The Ampersand*. After being sacked from this Dickensian firm of solicitors, 'as

---

[1] *Common's Luck* (producer John Mapplebeck), BBC TV, first transmitted on 25 June 1974.
[2] George Orwell, 'Authentic Socialism', *New English Weekly* (16 June 1938), p. 192.
[3] Jack Common Collection, 151: diary, 19 April 1950.

a scapegoat', he spent three years on the dole, and then in 1928 left for London, a 'poorly educated, dialect-speaking, recently unemployed member of the working class'.[4] Taken up there by John Middleton Murry, he worked on *The Adelphi*, and struck up a close friendship with Orwell.[5] During the 1930s he developed a considerable talent as an essayist, forging a style that would be true to his working-class point of view and way of speech. After the war, as the father of a large family, he was forced for reasons of economic survival to take on a succession of odd jobs, labouring and working as a script writer and literary advisor for various film companies. The first novel particularly was written under severely adverse circumstances; physically exhausting manual labour during the day, and soul-destroying hackwork on film reports during the evening: only the weekends were left for novel-writing. As his friend Tommy McCulloch put it, 'his life was struggle, struggle, struggle'.[6] That anything was produced at all is in itself an achievement; that something of the worth of *Kiddar's Luck* should have been produced – on the whole a qualitatively superior novel to the second – is a testimony to Common's energy and will. Gradually, however, the drain on his creative talents took its toll, and after the mid 1950s he produced virtually nothing of significance. He died in 1968, his work largely unrecognized.

There are two distinct and separate phases in Jack Common's writing career: the political essays of the 1930s, and the fictional work of the 1950s. In this essay we shall concentrate on the novels. Like many other working-class writers before and since, Common turned in the post-war period to an exploration of his own past and identity through the form of autobiography. In so doing, he was seeking to understand, in Roy Pascal's phrase, the 'successive collisions with circumstances' through which his own fate and destiny were woven, for the autobiographical form is that which documents more than any other the interaction of self and social context: 'the operation of spirit upon circumstances, as well as that of circumstances upon spirit'.[7]

For the working-class writer the autobiographical project and genre have assumed a particularly important role. David Vincent has recently documented one important period in the long tradition of autobiographical writing in which working-class men and women have struggled 'to grasp imaginatively the complexity of the lifelong interactions between the self and the outside world'.[8] Autobiography – a form of expression that has been neglected by commentators on working-class culture – affords many fruitful points of access in attempting to understand the constitution of the

[4]Jack Common, 'Orwell at Wallington', *Stand* (22 March 1981), p. 35.
[5]For an account of Common's experience of Orwell see his 'Orwell at Wallington'. For Orwell's letters to Common, see Sonia Orwell and Ian Angus, eds., *The Collected Essays, Journalism and Letters of George Orwell* 1 (London, Penguin, 1971). See also Bernard Crick, *George Orwell – A Life* (London, Secker and Warburg, 1980).
[6]*Common's Luck*.
[7]Roy Pascal, *Design and Truth in Autobiography* (Cambridge, Mass., Harvard U.P., 1960), pp. 2, 96.
[8]David Vincent, *Bread, Knowledge and Freedom* (London, Europa, 1981), p. 6.

individual human subject within the class and patriarchal structure of social relations. In his novels, particularly *Kiddar's Luck*, Jack Common succeeds in fashioning a particularly sensitive working-class vision within the autobiographical mode. What Common does is to marry literary technique and style, in this process of retrospection, with certain qualities and features of popular oral cultural expression, ranging from the commonplace but localized traditions of repartee and kidding, through the idiomatic narratives of the raconteur and folk-tale teller, to the more formal characteristics of monologue recitation and stand-up comic turns. Throughout Common's fiction, there is the constant interweaving of a self-conscious literariness with the oral and colloquial tones still flourishing in his native region during the period of his upbringing (markedly, for example, in the north-eastern music hall, as well as in everyday vernacular speech). Particularly characteristic of this is the distinctive irony, humour and self-mockery of *Kiddar's Luck* and *The Ampersand*. There is that same distancing through humour that has, as Martha Vicinus suggests with reference to nineteenth-century street literature, provided the working-class voice both with a source of self protection and resistance, and also with a sense of mutual encouragement, solidarity and community.[9] Ironic humour is in fact a distinctive tone of proletarian class- and self-consciousness, expressing moods that range from laconic resignation to buoyant self-confidence and pride. It is precisely this humour and irony that allow Common (like the working-class raconteur) to explore his own life at a distance and for its generality; Common is just as much interested in the representative nature of his fate as in his own unique and particular circumstances. And it is this humorous strain, too, along with other diverse influences of popular culture, that allows Common to solve the problem (in part at least) of finding an appropriate working-class literary style and tone, a problem which is, as Hoggart has noted, more difficult for the working classes than for writers from more privileged backgrounds.[10] It is, for instance, the use of this humorous tone in *Kiddar's Luck* that allows the writer to 'switch angles, to use a saving irony towards the self',[11] and thereby to lay down one important characteristic strand in establishing an idiom of class self-expression and analysis.

Both *Kiddar's Luck* and *The Ampersand* are, then, strongly autobiographical. Virtually 'all the background facts in Kiddar are true'[12] – the account of his family and friends, his street, school and neighbourhood, is solidly based on his own childhood experience. Similarly, much of the detail in *The Ampersand* comes from Common's own past life: the accounts of college and work are derived from his own experience at Skerry's College and at the solicitor's office in Newcastle where he gained his first job. But it should be noted that the two texts are autobiographical in different ways. Although unfortunately he did not elaborate, it is to this

[9]Martha Vicinus, *The Industrial Muse* (London, Croom Helm, 1974), pp. 29, 32, 38.
[10]Richard Hoggart, *Speaking to Each Other* (London, Penguin, 1973) II, p. 185.
[11]Op. cit., p. 175.
[12]Lyall Wilkes, *Tyneside Portraits* (Newcastle upon Tyne, Frank Graham, 1971), p. 155.

difference that Common was presumably intimating when he wrote that the second novel is 'not a truthful autobiography to be read in the same tone of voice required for the Kiddar'.[13] *Kiddar's Luck* is more consistently autobiographical: here Common is drawing upon an established tradition of autobiographical writing about childhood; Pascal suggests that autobiographies of childhood all display a great similarity.[14] In the second novel, however, Common finds the autobiographical form less wieldly – note the switch from first- to third-person narrative – and fictional and novelistic elements here bulk larger.

If autobiographical expression is common to both texts, it must be stressed that both are not simply and straightforwardly autobiographical; they are autobiographical *novels*. In neither does Common allows himself to be limited by the genre of autobiography. He freely fictionalizes parts of his life and combines this with invented detail and story. The virtue for Common of writing an autobiographical novel lay in the potential it gave him for giving its sequence of events a symbolic resonance, for revealing aspects of past life which at the time were submerged and latent, and which the autobiography with its main emphasis on chronological narrative and surface action is not so well equipped, formally, to explore. Autobiographical novelists are free to invent, where appropriate, in order to explore all the covert possibilities of their material, and artistic invention means they can attempt to get inside other people as well as outside themselves. As Roy Pascal puts it: 'Life must restrict in a thousand ways, and without the resources of invention, of art, we should remain ignorant of much that is decisive in man. If one remains true to the facts, too much eludes'.[15]

Drawing upon the conventions and traditions of autobiographical writing, the novels chart the transition from childhood through youth to early manhood. The narrative of both novels is concerned with the working-class version of this trajectory, documenting the passage from the relative freedom and hopes of a particular working-class childhood to the constraints, limitations and disillusionment of a life of labour. What we are presented with is a proletarian reworking of the romantic image of a fall from innocence to experience. The underlying theme is that of a transition from freedom to necessity; from the pre-eminence of the pleasure principle to that of the reality principle, which – as Freud argued – 'is one of the most important steps forward in the ego's development': the two novels dramatize the process of socialization whereby the proletarian ego is 'slowly educated by the pressure of external necessity to appreciate reality and obey the reality principle'.[16] The encounter of Will Kiddar/Clarts with 'the instructress necessity' is the major component of both these autobiographical texts. This central motif then becomes the axis

[13]Jack Common Collection, 136: letter to Michael Hodson of the Turnstile Press, 5 January 1954.
[14]Pascal, p. 84.
[15]Op. cit., p. 177 and chapter 11 passim.
[16]Sigmund Freud, *The Complete Introductory Lectures on Psychoanalysis* (London, George Allen & Unwin, 1971), pp. 357, 371.

around which a number of opposing and conflicting elements are woven into the thematic and narrative texture of the novels. Childhood pleasure in particular is conceived as the realm of innocence and imagination, of freedom, timelessness and play, of fellowship and community. What intervenes and destroys this childhood realm is time and time-discipline; the passage of time, growing up, becomes synonymous with the increasing limitation of freedom, disenchantment from communality, the imposition of work and the subordination of pleasure to destiny, fate, necessity. The pleasure–reality antinomy is thus seen, from this working-class perspective, above all in terms of a profound disjunction between play and work, between a realm of imaginative exploration, creativity and communal life, and a socially divisive, dehumanizing structure of relations and regimented action, extrinsic to people's control and intrinsically hostile to a truly popular aesthetics. The aim of this short essay is to explore how these key thematic elements are deployed, in concrete terms, in the unfolding of the narrative.

For Common, it was the local streets of Heaton in Newcastle that provided the most significant context in which the freedom of childhood was experienced. Early in *Kiddar's Luck* he powerfully evokes an almost mystical experience of infancy when, crawling about the pavement near his home, raindrops 'like pennies came splashing down, patterning the light summer pavement with dark discs, and faster, wetting my hands, my hair, my back – I chuckled over the lovely pennies'. Of this 'pavement-memory' he says – 'it was one of those moments, brief and trivial in themselves, for which time's clock stops. The only reason why they are indelible that I can see, is that in them everything stood still suddenly and all things were equally aware, not selecting, willing, making. Everything was in being, that only. And being is not transient' (16). Though rather less momentously, this sense of freedom was perpetuated in the life and culture of the streets, particularly in the 'child-community' (17) and the 'genial company' (19) which he found there. The street was his 'second home' where he was 'pavement-free and pal-pleasured' (19): 'Though for some time mainly passive among its activities, I had the freedom of it by right and could come into its full heritage whenever I was able' (16). This feeling of belonging to the street was enjoyed as a right, and understood as a 'social certitude' (19) invulnerable to the buffetings of domestic stress (particularly the effects on the family of his mother's drinking, and his parents' slowly disintegrating marriage). The sense of close fellowship among corner-lads continued throughout childhood. The pleasure of games among 'marble millionaires' (37); the anarchy of street play, daubing the door-handles of shops with sticks dipped in shit-buckets (59); the street practice of 'yarning and speculating about life, particularly the life they would have when they left school and were real working-men' (37): these are typical examples of how corner-lads were drawn together in the cohesion of an intimate group and an indigenous street-culture.

But Common's youthful enjoyment of freedom, community and imaginative life was of course finite; overshadowing it was the fate circumscribing the adult lives of all working-class people and fellow kiddars. Retrospectively he felt 'doomed' from the very moment he was born into a working-class family, for the short, sweet taste of the street's cultural heritage was contested by the experience of a totally opposed working-class heritage: work, boredom, subservience, unfreedom. 'Mind-forged manacles', oppressive forces, came increasingly to constrain the working-class child, materially and culturally. In an ironic passage, Common speculates upon how, before birth, a rich array of possibilities lay before 'me and my genes', with 'the whole world of chance open to us. It was then we made a mess of things': 'In the back-bedroom of an upstairs flat in a street parallel with the railway line . . . I chose my future parents. There, it was done . . . I at once came under the minus-sign which society had already placed upon my parents. . . . A sad mistake; though millions make it I think it still deserves a mourning wreath' (5–6). From this moment on the die is cast. Common's fate is overlooked by bad fairies: 'One, somewhat like a tramp, chalked upon the bedstead the sign which means "No hand-outs here"; another, four-belted as a ghostly navvy, swung his pick in promise of future hard work; a blear-eyed one, faintly lit up, lifted the bottle; and one looking like a magistrate made a bitter mouth over the syllables of an unspoken "Borstal" ' (6). As Common says in his parodic use of the letter of application for work in the closing pages of the first novel: 'It is usual to enclose testimonials as to one's good behaviour and ability when asking for a job. I send my horoscope instead. What is important about a man is not how able he is, nor how hard-working, but what's his luck' (144). Throughout the novels we are acutely aware of the fate or luck that overhangs the lives of kiddars all, the 'unprofitable heredity' and the 'stony environment' (145). For Common, the 'curse that dogged his family' (241) was to be working class, and to be working class was understood in terms of doomed luck or fate, a conception in the novels which moves, for different characters, between a kind of gritty realism and a politically disabling superstition.

The agent of fate is time; it is time that will inevitably deliver Kiddar to his destiny. The first novel begins outside of time, with Common's genes 'hanging about on the other side of time' (5). But this 'comer from eternity' (7) becomes of necessity drawn into mortal time: the moment of his birth is referred to as 'the small tick of my earliest animation' (79). And forebodingly, 'the clock struck nine as I gave my first yell' (8). During the brief spell of childhood freedom, though, time is held in abeyance, childhood is marked as the aftermath of timelessness and eternity: 'the hours of childhood ripen as slowly as plums upon a wall and the sun often stands for hours in the sky when children play' (125). Yet time and clocks are ominously present in the household of Common's infancy. Describing another poignant and mystical moment of infancy, Common describes the confrontation of ecstasy and time. He recalls 'the magnificent array of aspidistras and scented geranium which fringed the southward looking window. They made wonderful patterns of green light on the bit of floor under the clock – my favourite place for sitting on the pot. I must have looked a sort of gremlin child perched there directly under the clock, a green geranium-filtered light about me' (11–22). *Kiddar's Luck* is marked by the incessant ticking away of time. The end of infancy is signalled by entrance into school, and this first initiation into the discipline of social reality is later paralleled by the transition to work, which finally and irrevocably cuts 'the navel-cord attaching me to my childhood' (141). At this moment, 'when my clock threatened to strike fourteen', Common was destined to take his 'debut on the stage of full manhood' (123): there was a pull on 'so many of us to put away childish things and go to be little men together in the greater world of work' (135). Common describes himself at this stage of his life as 'one of the company of time-travellers' (124), about to disappear 'over time's weir' (125). This innocence became dissipated in the knowledge of 'this world of time and crumbling days' (8). He had then to accommodate himself to the real world and its demands. Both novels gravitate around the tragi-comic struggle to confront the passing of time and the transition from innocence and freedom to experience and necessity, a struggle which is marked most of all by the hero's attempt to 'regain a world relatively innocent of the ticking clock and of the measured out values, human and material, that tick is the ready symbol of' (36).

At the other end of the tunnel of time in *Kiddar's Luck* is the oncoming express-train of work. The degrading and dull compulsion of proletarian labour is the 'real world' to which working-class children must accommodate themselves, a world of 'hard graft and sweat-rag realism' (154). This process involves a time-journey from the organic time of childhood – 'childhood's time is biological, its seasons move like eras and are counted among the creeping changes of the physical climate which successively cloud and crystallize in mannikin shapes about the young identity' (50) – to the mechanical time of adulthood where kiddars confront their 'heritage, the routine of the factory or some similar industrial hour-glass regularly turning the sands of uncelebrated and nearly unconsequenced labour' (141). It is in *The Ampersand* that work is discussed most fully; in *Kiddar's Luck* it remains a ghostly, but ever-looming presence. *Kiddar's Luck* concentrates on the apprenticeship into working-class life, Common's experience of moving 'through a looking glass into the real world beyond' (51), and it documents two key agents of enculturation and accommodation to the reality principle: the father and the school. *Kiddar's Luck* is the saga of young Common's jousting with these forces of otherness, discipline, authority, the forces that seek to stifle his sense of pleasure, play and freedom.

Significantly, the father, a domineering figure with 'his strange masculine power' (23), is *ab initio* associated with time, reality and the containment of pleasure. As a railwayman his life is centred around time – 'a man of trains and punctually achieved destinations' (26) – and a regular domestic occupation of his is cleaning the many clocks in the house: 'clocks were very much his perquisite; nobody dreamt of touching them either in his presence or absence' (122). At the time of Kiddar's birth, the father's role as guardian of time and of the principle of reality is made crystal clear: 'Father heard me, heard the clock, thought that sounds like a boy and that clock's fast. He was right in both suppositions' (9). His immediate act is to put the clock right: 'At least he'd start me running on time' (9). This obeisance to clocks and timetables is contrasted particularly with the attributes of his mother, a creature of introspection and soured imagination. At the time of Common's job-hunting, his mother 'sat by the fire poking the dead ashes away and she could see it, she could see the brightness coming, surely, but not how or when. 'That's all granny', said my father, who looked at the clock, not at the hot crumbling of coals, and knew that the travelling minute brings the hour up, when it strikes, what you've done, you've done, no reward to the idler'. (133–4)

As a child, the lad sees his own anger as 'male like my father's', while his fear is associated with his mother (79). The father is a symbol of patriarchal authority, the mother of imagination and the inability to negotiate reality, and it is naturally the father who disciplines the child. An early infant game of 'pretend' is rudely interrupted by the father who 'came in to see what was what, saw, flew into a rage and began thrashing me' (13). The young lad's truancy from school is likewise marked by a thrashing from his father: 'It was severe, but that didn't matter. It was cold-blooded, unprovoked, and carried out by a man whose unease was not the heat of anger nor anything that my small experience recognized, so there was a shock in it' (35). The father and the male teachers he subsequently encounters are the agents of patriarchal order. None the less, the father acts ambivalently, for although he must act as the agent of social control he experiences a painful internal conflict: he was 'wrong, utterly wrong inside. He had blacklegged his own best impulse, and for such as he, blacklegging of any kind, not rebellion, is the major crime' (35). Kiddar understands that the father is fulfilling a function demanded of him by the social order – that of turning out a son able to cope with the world as it actually exists. So when the son seeks to take over the role of his mother, who struggles inadequately to keep the house in order, his father lambasts him as 'a Jessie, a little girl doing mammy's housework': 'he was right of course. I had the instinct to feel that. Not even for the purest of motives is it good to make a lassie of yourself if you aren't one by nature' (80). Socialized into the iron-fast conventions of working-class gender roles, the boy comes to accept that this is, in one sense, as things must be: it is the nature of things. The father dispels his mother's inadequacy and sense of fear: 'one could sleep safe if he was there' (40). And he simply overrides his 'mother's opinions and doubts and worries . . . as he did my own waywardness' (23). Thus, the lad comes to be included in 'the masculine conspiracy against woman' (47; also 167). Yet it should be stressed that the paternal–maternal symbolical divide is not at all times clear-cut, for his father is occasionally and potentially open to the power of imagination, as for example in his reading of comics with his son (26–7), or in his vicarious experience of the mental adventures of book-learning (171). The father has a residual sense of imagination, and he too was for a time 'living imaginatively in their son's future as she loved to do' (171). The point is that this patriarchal order and its insistence on subordination to the dull compulsion of economic reality ensure that his creative potential remains embryonic and crippled.[17]

Kiddar's father is, however, only one agent of time-discipline and the denial of imagination; he hands on the baton of authority to the school. As with the father, so too is the school a custodian of time: 'Nine till twelve, two to four or four-thirty, these were the hours of petrification' (84). School is the place of 'regular-attendance-and-punctuality' (82), the place of boredom, of serving time. Kiddar acquires 'the one faculty with which every school infallibly endows its pupils, that of being bored. It is very important, of course, that every child should in the course of time become fitted up with this negative capability. If they didn't have it they'd never put up with the jobs they are going to get, most of them, on leaving school. Boredom, or the ability to endure it, is the hub on which the whole universe of work turns' (32). In a damning indictment of working-class schooling, Common suggests that the function of school is to make it 'quite certain you can put us to the most boring job there is and we'll endure it' (33). In the process of being schooled, most children find the curriculum itself to be 'a bit of a conundrum' (83), unable to cater for those who had already internalized the reality that 'we're going to be just ordinary workers'. School equals 'pointlessness' (84): 'As for your future prospects, well, in any case, the possibility was that you would be going into a job very like the one your old man had – you didn't want to be too bright for that' (87).

School means oppression. Its function is to instil discipline and respect for authority. For example, Mr Gillespie, the headmaster, was in his anger 'a pretty terrible figure': 'Experts testified that he could put more sting into a lashing than any other teacher in the town' (126). School suppressed what for Common were the supreme qualities of childhood – innocence and imagination – and whereas with most working-class children this process is more or less efficient, the dampening of Kiddar's imaginative faculties is felt particularly poignantly and acutely, and the resistance is particularly spirited. His time at school amounts to a 'permanent state of rebellion against the discipline and dullness of lessons' (126). By the time he enters Skilbeck's Commercial College he is of course in many ways a different person; he has for example by then developed a 'new alert sense of the real in his world', and 'before that his ego dwindled' (195). Nevertheless he continues to chafe at the 'greater and lesser boredoms which dotted the day', and which he 'evaded or enlivened . . . according to the promptings of a fluctuating ingenuity'. His ambition on entering college transfers itself 'to the more customary habit of dreams' (172), yet there is as well open rebellion, as in his clash with the utilitarian ethos and mentality of the school (see 191–203), and in his truancy from the end-of-year exams

---

[17]We are not of course claiming that Common stood in the vanguard of feminism. He was in many ways a characteristic male-centred working-class socialist of his generation. What we are claiming is that his fiction implicitly reveals how gender identities are shaped in working-class life (see also *Revolt Against an Age of Plenty*, pp. 73–4), and that his appreciation of his mother's foibles as portrayed in the two novels is sensitive and penetrating.

(219–21). Basically, because 'unwarmed by his imagination', college 'remained a mere mechanical set of circumstances, the way work so often is to the long-practised adult' (217).[18]

Common's early experience of school was marked by the contrast of lessons with playtime when 'the screw was loosened' (84). During this period a sense of freedom, pleasure and vitality of imagination was rekindled – 'the ossification of the spirit of play had not yet set in . . . there was no compulsion about what we did then' (85). And, of course, at the end of the school day 'we were free again and the streets were ours' (87). This dualism of time and experience was not enough however and Will could not submit to the discipline of lessons: 'The least departure from routine was welcome' (85). This was often stimulated by a 'collective naughtiness' (36). The major manifestation of Common's rebelliousness at school was his truancy – a period of 'glorious freedom' (33). The outcome was retrospectively to emphasize the conflict between freedom and authority. Will and his friends are caught and 'some bright little man, hard inside with the boredom of his own upbringing, gave it as his opinion that I needed discipline. Discipline, why certainly, all agreed to that. Discipline, oh yes, blessed stuff that even the meanest who ever got in a position of authority are always ready to give away with both hands. Discipline, nod, nod, social cement – stick it on the rebellious till they stiffen' (34–5). However, the experience is rich:

> By self-inflicted outlawry one can gain a world relatively innocent of the ticking clock and of the measured out values, human and material, that tick is the ready symbol of. . . . For the period of your freedom, *you have been an outsider to whom the contrived universe of the socially included is a curiosity*. Afterwards, its compulsions will always lack the final validity; you'll keep somewhere in you a useful incredulity which is really a readiness to welcome the coming of livelier customs that haven't had the spring worn out of them by the bottom of their sit-pretties. [36, our emphasis]

At this point Will moves beyond the simple dualism between freedom (the streets) and boredom (school). He seeks to turn his experience of school into one of freedom, to distance himself from the discipline. But the price of dislocating himself from the given is outlawry.

Thus far we have come upon Will's capacity for imagination in two ways. Firstly, we have seen the natural, spontaneous imagination of childhood. This is the unalloyed pleasure of street life, a world of timeless and 'communal inventiveness. This aspect of Will's existence continues some way into adolescence with the local street gangs and their battles. It is

---

[18]Like the father and the teacher, so too is religion the agent of power, authority and patri-archal discipline. Common is introduced early on to 'God's anger against the wicked' (43), and he becomes aware that religion encourages a sense of servitude and the 'withering of the communal spirit' (80).

present most notably in 'The Sons of the Battle Axe', a gang in which Common and his mates 'were Norsemen, the last company of Vikings, surviving in the sign of our Battle-axe. And then we were international crooks' (103). These acts of play articulated a public and communal life.

The second source of Common's exceptional imaginative existence lay in his rejection of the discipline and boredom of public reality. In the novels this occurs in three ways. Firstly, in the negative rejection of the existing social order through the act of truancy. A second and similarly negative, though distinct, consequence of his thwarted freedom to inhabit the potential space between individual and environment, wherein cultural creativity arises, is manifested in the socially deviant activity of fiddle and theft. As his imaginative life becomes increasingly privatized, so he moves beyond the communally-orientated shoplifting sanctioned in the street-corner culture into an individual pathology of solitary stealing. The genesis of juvenile 'delinquent' behaviour has been the subject of considerable dispute since at least the time of the Hooligans, and no doubt will continue to be, but Common's autobiographical novels do at least provide us with a vivid and cogent portrayal of how the need for a resource or relatively free behaviour pattern enjoyed earlier in life 'may reappear at a later age when deprivation threatens',[19] and if fulfilment of this need is obstructed, how it may become manifest in other ways, less personally or culturally rewarding and often ideologically labelled as deviant.

Thirdly, Kiddar escapes more and more into his own imaginative life. Reading becomes particularly important to him, and he delights in reading ' "liars", *Magnet, Gem, Boy's Friend, Buffalo Bill, Robin Hood*' (86; cf. 26). Will could even get some mileage out of the Bible: 'I actually read the thing, right through, cover to cover as if it was *Chips* or *Hereward the Wake*' (45). But this world, upon which he is increasingly forced back, is more ambivalent, for it is a realm of private existence, compensating for his growing alienation from the communal life of the street. This is made apparent from early on where the story telling is associated with the mother and fear of the social world of reality: 'we were both safe before our fireside, she could . . . take pleasure in my eager response to the stories she told me' (19). Invariably her stories tended towards nostalgia, the dream of unfulfilled hopes and aspirations ship-wrecked on the reefs of (male-dominated) reality. She gazed into the fire and 'told of the balls she'd been to and how pretty all said she was, rather like an ex-Cinderella whom the Prince had discarded in early middle-age and who sat at the hopeless hearth now, forlorn of fairyland' (39). Common's mother was a 'connoisseur of dreams' (89), but of dreams that failed to negotiate with the real world and which marginalized her female existence.

The creative and imaginative life becomes a problem in the novels because of its solitariness, its inner nature. Most of Will's peers move from the *communal* existence of the streets to the *communal* world of work and are prepared to sacrifice the imaginative life: 'Anyone who still had some

[19]D.W. Winnicott, *Playing and Reality* (London, Tavistock Publications, 1971), p. 4.

toys left raffled them off. Certain celebrated collections of *Magnets* and *Gems*, of cigarette cards, marbles, were hurriedly discarded. . . . On the corners there was a continual series of "dares" running on, not on the old follow-my-leader kind of thing, but a measuring up of individual in man-to-man competition. And one and all seemed to have picked a job for themselves: they knew what they were going to be' (135). Will seeks to retain the imaginative *freedom* of the streets, but in so doing he sacrifices communal existence for the *private* and solitary life – 'the more private play of fantasy' (60). Increasingly he becomes 'uncomfortably aware that there were attractions upon me that pulled in unknown directions and threatened to take me out of the orbit my fellow corner-lads so naturally swung into. My enthusiasms were beginning to strike them as too intense' (127). It becomes apparent to the other lads 'that I had a life of my own that they wouldn't want to share, particularly not now when they were entering upon an early manhood that they most decidedly wanted to be orthodox' (127). Will's imaginative existence becomes a 'secret life' (127); he is described as 'riding the impossible abysses of past ages', his eyes 'drugged with in-seeing' (128). In *The Ampersand* it is said retrospectively that he 'succeeded in keeping the harsh realities of the corner lad's existence at bay by constantly reading or contriving fictions. All his comings and goings, battles and defeats, were attended by a running commentary which softened and interpreted events so that his dream-personality could continue to flourish over them' (153). Will's dream personality and self-glorifying personae drown out reality (as with his mother): they 'deepened my introspection' and 'took me further away from my own generation' (139). Will's imagination and striving for freedom force him more and more into a lonely existence. He walks the streets of Newcastle, travelling 'along the empty streets into the crowds and out again' (128). No longer are these the streets of his childhood freedom. His only contact with the working class is to jostle with the crowd on Saturday night. His isolation deepens even more following his eventual rejection of the conventions (in prospect) of a traditional working-class marriage; he separates from Mabel his girlfriend and announces to her: 'I've got to go a different way to the folks round here. I'm not meant for this kind of life' (297). Will has become an outsider, an outlaw. His only consolation is the idea of a 'special destiny'. This private imaginative life has drowned out all reality and flooded his being.

Kiddar sees the implication of this direction and predicament embodied in the figure of the eccentric uncle of both the novels. This uncle is an atheist, socialist, vegetarian and crank. As a working-class intellectual, he is an anomaly, leading a life 'obstinately different from the working class households all around' (136). In this situation he lives 'unnaturally' alone: marginalized, isolated, wifeless. Kiddar identifies with his eccentricity, and admires his valuable and original qualities, but in the end he refuses the alternative route which his uncle represents. His conclusion is that 'a working class crank was really a kind of city-idiot, tolerated and laughed at' (186). Such a person follows his own individual bent at the expense of not belonging to his kind; his freedom has been bought at the cost of a quasi-anchoretic severance from the community around him. The working man who in any way uproots himself is 'as much a living anomaly as the wealthy priest, the socially-approved poet, the knighted socialist, or the bearded lady' (143). Kiddar therefore rejects his uncle's solution to the central struggle between self and the constraints of the external social world underlying both the novels.

The central action of both novels is one individual's fateful struggle during childhood and adolescence to negotiate the interaction between subjective and imaginative experience, and the necessities of the external world. The psychoanalyst Donald Winnicott has written about this problem in a way which very usefully illuminates Common's fictional representation of it. Particularly relevant is his identification of the location of cultural experience. For Winnicott, the process of weaning for the infant involves a fundamental 'disillusion' – literally dis-illusion-ment – a realization of an independent external world he or she cannot control imaginatively. Here begins accommodation to the reality principle. What Winnicott refers to as 'transitional phenomena' – bits of cloth, blankets, toys, even 'a word or tune' – are a child's initial means of negotiating the 'intermediate area between the subjective and that which is objectively perceived'.[20] The use of a transitional object is the infant's first step on a 'journey from the purely subjective' towards experience of objective reality. But this journey is never finally concluded during life, for 'no human being is free from the strain of relating inner and outer reality', and as relief from this strain, recourse is had to 'an intermediate area of experience', a 'potential space' of freedom and creativity.[21] It is here, according to Winnicott, that cultural and aesthetic experience is located, and in the healthy individual there is, or ideally should be, a direct line of continuity between transitional phenomena, childhood play, and adult cultural creativity.[22] By extension, we can also say that the health of a culture, in this sense, is predicated upon the degree to which this intermediate area of creative freedom is allowed and nourished.

For Common, this fundamental space, enjoyed in childhood games and street play, is betrayed by the central socializing agents of a patriarchal and capitalist social order. The reality of working-class labour and the masculine world in their demands upon a person is profoundly antithetical to the aesthetic, imaginative and playful dimension of human development and creativity. The effect this has on Kiddar is increasingly to transmute his healthy imaginative powers (allied to the positive process of dreaming, which facilitates object-relating in the real world), into the disabling act of fantasying. While imaginative expression and aesthetic response are in certain ways repressed by the motivating forces and institutional processes of a capitalist social formation, fantasying represents a failure to negotiate the problems of the external social world, and involves, in greater or lesser

[20] Op. cit., p. 3.
[21] Op. cit., pp. 13, 100.
[22] Op. cit., see chapter 7.

degree, dissociation from that world. As Winnicot puts it, fantasying is compulsive, it has 'no poetic value, whereas dream does', and it 'interferes with action and with life in the real or external world', as well as with 'personal or inner psychic reality, the living core of the individual personality'.[23] Though it is an unwitting attempt to regain a lost creative freedom, Kiddar's retreat into fantasy is confirmed and increased as the spontaneous imagination of childhood fades.

What real and viable solution is there, then, for Kiddar? Cursed with the bad luck of a working-class fate; alienated from his own kind by the world of books and learning, and by his own self-aggrandizing fictions; the solution of 'crankihood' cast aside; the contemporary practice and institutional forms of religion rejected (80–1); a future of alienated labour and claustrophobic domesticity refused – Kiddar's predicament reflects that of any working-class person who attempts on his or her own to bend the bars of patriarchal and capitalist servitude. The logic of the social order decrees distinct and unyielding roles and functions. *Kiddar's Luck* and *The Ampersand* dramatize the refusal and questioning of that order, not in the dutiful name of revolution and class consciousness, but in the name of a dimly perceived order that would transcend the barbarity of partriarchal capitalism in the name of a radically other social order, one that is regulated in the name of imagination, creativity and freedom. It is in the remembered experience of childhood and its potentiality that Common – like Blake or Wordsworth before him – forges the intellectual tools to explore that possibility. In *Kiddar's Luck* this quest is unfulfilled, and Kiddar must accommodate himself to the dictates of reality. But there remains – in the ironic tones of Will's final letter of application for a job – a note of defiance, challenge and distantiation: 'So far I cannot claim to have experienced any exceptionally untoward event which might suggest that I'm a destined child of fortune. Nevertheless, as it is high time the luck of the Kiddars turned, that goes for all of them, I intend to live in every possible way as if it had; and to regard any unblessed existence such as most kinds of work still are, as worth only a temporary endurance' (145). As an outsider, a social outlaw, Kiddar must always question 'the contrived universe of the socially included'; for him, henceforth, 'its compulsions will always lack the final validity', and he will retain a 'useful incredulity' (36). Similarly, in *The Ampersand* the central figure remains an outsider, a delinquent fleeing from the social order. The novel fittingly ends on a note of doubt and uncertainty, an indeterminate future ahead as Kiddar escapes from the trammels of the past. As he leaves home in the early dawn, the family cat follows him along the walls of the back-lane until they reach the bottom: 'That was far enough for the cat evidently. It stayed on the top of the last coal-house roof, calling no more but its curved tail wavering up in a small question-mark abrupt against the risen sun' (310).

That same question-mark always hovered over Jack Common's own fate. Once he left Heaton and his roots, seeking to deploy his undoubted skills

---

[23]Op. cit., pp. 31, 35, and chapter 2 passim.

as a writer, he experienced the vicissitudes reserved for those who seek to move beyond their allotted place in the social and cultural order. Taken up temporarily by Middleton Murry at *The Adelphi*, as much for his authentic class background as for his undeniable abilities, Common inevitably became a 'living anomaly' like his fictional uncle. A recipient of middle-class patronage and interest, yet unable to assimilate himself fully into the cultural milieu of the world of letters, Common's fate was to live a precarious and often destitute life – the fate of so many social and cultural migrants. Existing within the no-man's land between classes and cultures, Common suffered much anguish, despair and self-doubt in achieving what he did. It is a just measure of his abilities that he succeeded in combating penury and hardship to produce that 'mixture of messianic hope and cheerful pessimism' that George Orwell found in his writing.[24] Freud once wrote that 'a piece of creative writing, like a daydream, is a continuation of, and a substitute for, what was once the play of childhood':[25] the achievement of Jack Common resides, just so, in the way he turned his childhood vision and creativity into the imaginative pursuit of freedom in *Kiddar's Luck* and *The Ampersand*.

These novels are a rare and important achievement within the canon of working-class writing, and a valuable alternative and corrective to the tradition of orthodox 'proletarian fiction'. What we have in these texts is an account of a working-class odyssey through the cultural and social order, tracing the transformation from the creative anarchy of childhood to the disenchanted and dis-illusioned drudgery of proletarian subordination. And it is, as such, also a narrative of the construction of masculine, and feminine, identities within the patriarchal order, the one representing rationality and reality, the other the foundation of imaginative and creative life. Kiddar's story is that of the individual who kicks against the pricks, who challenges the fixing of patriarchal capitalist order and identity. In these autobiographical novels, Jack Common explores, in a humorous and uncompromising way, the forging of his own anomalous identity as a refugee between classes and cultures. Illuminating and infusing the whole narrative is Common's instinctive sense that there can be another – a radically other – social order of imaginative, creative and popular existence. And for this aspiration, Common – like many other writers – draws upon the utopian experience of childhood. For, Common argues in one of his essays, 'all the primary illusions, those which children have, those which come to people in love, those which float about the drinking-table, and those which simple people have concerning clever ones, are prophetic glances'.[26] What we all want, he goes on, 'is an illusion-becoming-fact, a sign in the heavens which like the high-blown gossamer of the dandelion seed is able to root in the earth and enrich it with a

[24]Orwell, 'Authentic Socialism', p. 192.
[25]Sigmund Freud, 'Creative Writers and Day-Dreaming', *Complete Works* (London, Hogarth Press, 1952) IX, p. 152.
[26]The Sweeper Up [Jack Common], 'A Shout up The Chimney', *The Adelphi* (December 1935), p. 178.

common homely gold'.[27] Common detects the stuff of socialism in the hopes, the illusions, of working-class people; these are the available ingredients for social transformation, and these seeds must be cultivated; 'Speaking generally, as a revolutionary materialist with a leg free, I'd say you can only abolish a persistent social illusion by making it fact'.[28] The fact of capitalism is to dis-illusion us; the fact of socialism must be to acknowledge and cultivate our illusions, imagination and sense of play. This vision, this aspiration to 'magic made material fact',[29] is the most abiding contribution of Jack Common to the tradition of working-class culture and literature.

[27]Op. cit.
[28]Op. cit.
[29]Op. cit.

Note

Most of Sillitoe's fiction is available in paperback reprint, under standard imprints (Star, Triad, etc.), and there would be little use in listing these separately.

The editions used of the main works discussed in this paper are as follows:

Saturday Night and Sunday Morning (London, W.H. Allen, 1958)
The Loneliness of the Long-distance Runner (London, W.H. Allen, 1959)
Key to the Door (London, W.H. Allen, 1961)
'The Good Women', *Daily Worker* (26 May – 2 June 1962)
The Ragman's Daughter (London, W.H. Allen, 1963)
The Death of William Posters (London, W.H. Allen, 1965)
A Tree on Fire (London, W.H. Allen, Star Books, 1979)
Guzman, Go Home (London, Pan Books, 1970)
A Start in Life (London, W.H. Allen, 1970)
Men Women and Children (London, W.H. Allen, 1973)
The Storyteller (London, W.H. Allen, Star Books, 1980)

Alan Sillitoe was born in Nottingham on 4 March 1928. When he was 14 he went to work as a labourer in a bicycle factory. When he was 17 he became an assistant air-traffic controller at a military airfield and a year later he enlisted in the Royal Air Force Voluntary Reserve as a wireless operator. From 1952 until 1958 he lived abroad in France, Italy, and Spain. In 1952 he married the poet Ruth Fainlight; they have two children. His first book of poems was published in 1957, his first novel in 1958, and since then he has published at least a book a year – poetry, novels, stories, plays, children's books, travel, essays. He was awarded the Hawthornden Prize in 1960. In 1970 he became Literary Adviser to W.H. Allen Ltd. During the sixties he wrote for the Anarchist paper *Freedom*, and belonged to CND. His home is at Wittersham in Kent.

Principal publications:

Saturday Night and Sunday Morning (London, W.H. Allen, 1958)
The Loneliness of the Long-distance Runner (London, W.H. Allen, 1959)
The General (London, W.H. Allen, 1960)
The Rats and other Poems (London, W.H. Allen, 1960)
Key to the Door (London, W.H. Allen, 1961)
The Ragman's Daughter (London, W.H. Allen, 1963)
A Falling Out of Love and other Poems (London, W.H. Allen, 1964)
The Road to Volgograd (London, W.H. Allen, 1964)
The Death of William Posters (London, W.H. Allen, 1965)
Love in the Environs of Voronezh (London, Macmillan, 1968)
Guzman, Go Home (London, Macmillan, 1968)
All Citizens Are Soldiers (with Ruth Fainlight: London, Macmillan, 1969)
A Start in Life (London, W.H. Allen, 1970)
Travels in Nihilon (London, W.H. Allen, 1971)
Raw Material (London, W.H. Allen, 1972)
Men Women and Children (London, W.H. Allen, 1973)
The Flame of Life (London, W.H. Allen, 1974)
Storm and other Poems (London, W.H. Allen, 1974)
The Widower's Son (London, W.H. Allen, 1976)
The City Adventures of Marmalade Jim (London, Robson, 1977)
The Storyteller (London, W.H. Allen, 1979)
The Second Chance (London, Jonathan Cape, 1981)
Her Victory (St Albans, Granada Publishing, 1982)
The Lost Flying Boat (London, Jonathan Cape, 1983)

7

The Roots of Sillitoe's Fiction

David Craig

I've only to say I hate Nottingham, he thought with a silent ironic laugh, for all the years it's put on me to come into my mind as clear as framed photos outside a picture house.[1]

This sentence from Alan Sillitoe's third novel expresses the thoughts of a character, Brian Seaton, and not the author's own. Yet it does suggest Sillitoe's conflicting views of the city where he grew up – the seed-bed of his experience. When he was asked at the Lancaster Literature Festival in 1982 what his old community thought of him, his reply was: 'I was asked once to a reception given by the Soviet Cultural Attaché in London, and there I met the Mayor of Nottingham. He didn't want to talk to me. They don't like what I've done.' Revulsion from the squalor and harshness of the old place – a deep-laid sense of its normality and homeliness and vigour: these two clusters of feelings are forever surfacing and going under again in Sillitoe's imagination, heating to boiling-point and dying away again. Working-class Nottingham comprises the gamut of human nature. It is what a free spirit is driven to flee from. Both these 'incompatible' attitudes lie at the root of his vision.

This vision (by which I mean an author's whole sense of the world and its possibilities) abides fairly unchanged through Sillitoe's work for 20 years, from the writing of the episodes that became *Saturday Night and Sunday Morning* to several of the key stories in *Men Women and Children* and even the very recent *The Storyteller*. Here is what Dickens might have called a 'keynote' passage from *Saturday Night*:

And trouble for me it'll be, fighting every day until I die. Why do they make soldiers out of us when we're fighting up to the hilt as it is? Fighting with mothers and wives, landlords and gaffers, coppers, army, government. . . . Born drunk and married blind, misbegotten into a strange and crazy world, dragged-up through the dole and into the war with a gas-mask on your clock, and the sirens rattling into you every

[1] Alan Sillitoe, *Key to the Door* (London, W.H. Allen, 1961), p. 241.

night while you rot with scabies in an air-raid shelter. Slung into khaki at eighteen, and when they let you out, you sweat again in a factory, grabbing for an extra pint, doing women at the weekend and getting to know whose husbands are on the night-shift. . . .[2]

This would at once be recognizable as Sillitoe. The prose moves with a headlong energy felt in the impact of the alliteration, the choice of a word like 'rattling' where a kind of heartfelt violence matters more than objective accuracy, the wish to generalize or opinionate which comes out in phrases only just enough removed from cliché to create specific meanings. Six years after that, in *The Death of William Posters*, Frank Dawley, factory worker on the run from his old life, says to a nurse who takes him in and gives him a meal:

Most of my mates wanted an easier job, less hours, more pay, naturally. But it wasn't really work they hated, don't think that. They didn't all want to be doctors or clerks, either. Maybe they just didn't like working in oil and noise, and then going home at night to a plate of sawdust sausages and cardboard beans, and two hours at the flicker-box with advertisements telling them that those sausages and beans burning their guts are the best food in the country. I don't suppose they knew what they wanted in most cases – except maybe not to be treated like cretins.[3]

This is a lucid, considered statement on behalf of his class. A little earlier in the same sequence, it has felt like this from the inside:

He was on the main road after the soldier's lift, doing ninety and dashing around like a tomcat after its own bollocks, tart wild and pub crazy after a stretch of high-fidelity that he'd stood so long because he was temporarily dead, thinking: 'I go round in circles, as if in some past time I've had a terrible crash, and the more I drive in circles the more I'm bleeding to death. I don't feel this bleeding to death because it's slow and painless (almost as if it's happening to another man and I'm not even looking on, but am reading about it in a letter from a friend hundreds of miles away) but I know it's happening because my eyes get tired and I'm fed up to my spinal marrow, while the old rich marrow I remember is withering and turning black inside me. . . .'[4]

The rough, ribald vernacular ingredient in this is still very much Arthur Seaton but the imagery symbolizing personal depths is more prominent than before and may represent an effort to act on some profound advice that David Storey had offered in a review of *The Ragman's Daughter* two years before:

[2]Alan Sillitoe, *Saturday Night and Sunday Morning* (London, W.H. Allen, 1958), p. 213.
[3]Alan Sillitoe, *The Death of William Posters* (London, W.H. Allen, 1965), p. 44.
[4]*Op. cit.*, p. 34.

In Sillitoe's work there is an ambiguity which is never resolved: the feeling that the revolution he would set up in society is in fact a revolution inside himself, and one which he has not yet acknowledged. Society – 'Them: The Rats' – is his externalising of something inside; a black and subtle aggression directed not against society but more truly against his own experience; his attempt to exorcise some incredible pain out there rather than within himself.[5]

In spite of this, the old ranting and railing at society, to say nothing of the old effort to define the real meanness in it, persists into the stories in *Guzman, Go Home*, especially 'Isaac Starbuck':

He turned north into the patchwork country. A rabbit-hutch bungalow stood for sale in a rabbit-food field. He imagined it worth three thousand pounds. Could get it for a couple of quid after the four-minute warning. Five bob, perhaps, as the owner runs terrified for the woods, hair greying at every step – if I wanted to own property and get a better deal in heaven.

Needle shivering at cold eighty, he felt something like love for the machine under him, the smooth engine swilled and kissed by oil, purring with fuel, cooled by the best water. Out of the rut of family, the trough of drink and the sud-skies of low-roofed factories. . . .[6]

Headlong he rushes past or away from the settled or average life, this hero (for the author allows little to qualify or resist him) who seethes with ungovernable energies that never find a way of gearing themselves to a fulfilling life.

These inseparable elements – the irrepressible urge to tear and break away, the feeling of unfulfilled personal powers – are as present as ever in *Men Women and Children*, especially in the earliest story and the latest, 'Before Snow Comes' (1967) and 'The Chiker' (1972). Mark, the hero of 'Before Snow Comes', hovers, as usual, on the border between settled, domestic life and an outcast limbo: he is divorced, and his love affair with Jean, a married woman, expires in a doomed way. At the core of his nature lies this typically embattled vision:

He worked at a cabinet-making factory as a joiner, making doors one week and window frames the next, lines of window frames and rows of doors. The bandsaws screamed all day from the next department like the greatest banshee thousand-ton atomic bomb rearing for the spot-middle of the earth which seemed to be his brain. Planing machines went like four tank engines that set him looking at the stone wall as if to see it keel towards him for the final flattening, and then the milling machines buzzing around like scout cars searching for the answers to all

[5]David Storey, 'Which revolution?', *The Guardian* (18 October 1963).
[6]'Isaac Starbuck', in Alan Sillitoe, *Guzman, Go Home* (London, Pan Books, 1970), p. 114.

questions. . . . It was like the Normandy battlefield all over again when he was eighteen, but without death flickering about. Not that noise bothered him, but he often complained to himself of minor irritations, and left the disasters to do their worst. It was like pinching himself to make sure he was alive.[7]

A 'chiker' is a peeping Tom, and Ken, who does the chiking, is a middle-aged man who rankles and smoulders at other people's sexual lives (his daughter and her boyfriend on the settee, young couples on the common at night): 'Maybe all men of his age felt young enough to be their own sons. . . . Now he was in the same boat and felt as if, on his way up through the orphanage and army, marriage and factory, he'd not been allowed to grow older properly like some people he knew.'[8] So he hotches to break out and away, and empathizes with unattached young men going towards the station with luggage in their hands. But he himself is embedded in habitual living (he works as a waste-paper baler in a factory) and his deep-seated conflict between rootedness and escape is caught in the terrific closing sequence where he goes berserk at the canary singing in his living-room, shoves it in its cage onto the fire-grate, and starts to kindle a fire under it. But he lets the match burn his fingers, opens the cage door, and sits there sobbing as the bird stops singing: 'He looked blankly at the bird and the wide open door of its cage, but it seemed as if it would never make a move. It sat on its perch and kept quiet, waiting for him to shut it before beginning its song again.'[9]

So the man (always the man) yearns to escape and harks back to his roots. Only five years ago the urge outwards (or drift south) was still the tendency of *The Storyteller*:

> He didn't know what had got him into such daftness. Telling tales in pubs! And for money? Show your teeth when you laugh like that, you ginger-haired bastard. Donkey-head. He lived a mile away, so the story of his story might not reach home. In any case they would be so drunk at chucking-out time that they wouldn't remember much of what happened by Sunday morning. You live in hope, but you die in squalor. Maybe he'd leave home, and do it in Leicester. Never cack on your own doorstep. Move South to Northampton and, after a week or two at the pubs there, go and cheer up the car workers of Luton, which would be good practice for when he finally chucked himself into London.[10]

This novel, however, strikes me as forced and over-written: few of the story-teller's stories could conceivably be delivered in any actual lounge or public

[7]'Before Snow Comes', in Alan Sillitoe, *Men Women and Children* (London, W.H. Allen, 1973), p. 68.
[8]'The Chiker', in Sillitoe, *Men Women and Children*, p. 146.
[9]*Op. cit.*, p. 155.
[10]Alan Sillitoe, *The Storyteller* (London, W.H. Allen, 1980), p. 37.

bar; and this is typical of the novels Sillitoe has written in the second part of his life, from *A Tree on Fire* through *A Start in Life* to *The Storyteller*. They tend to be horribly uncertain and fumbling, or lunging, in their touch. The Sillitoe who writes a sort of picaresque thriller set in the Home Counties in *A Start in Life* or a mixture of war novel and celebration of the Great Artist in *A Tree on Fire* no longer seems sure about what level he is working at or what voice to use. Characters are non-credible (e.g. John the mad radio genius in *A Tree on Fire*) even though the mode of the book is still apparently realism, and they are allowed to utter lengthy manifestoes or self-advertisements in the guise of lifelike dialogue. When we are most insistently invited to treat them as incarnations of vitality or creativity, we can only back away from their overweening egoism, or the implausibility with which it is dramatized. At the same time – for the past 19 years – he has never set a larger work in his old home community (although he has continued to use it for perfectly sure-footed short stories). The question I will try to answer in this essay is: has Sillitoe failed to make himself at home in any way of life other than his original one? Or to put it another way: are there shortcomings in his talent which can be overlaid by the sheer intimate knowledge of a place and its people but become glaring when he has to rely more on invention and less on memory?

The working class (those who live by the sale of their labour-power and draw no income from surplus-value created by others) make up three-quarters of the population of countries like ours. Yet such is the chronic cultural imbalance that working-class experience has always bulked little in our literature (at least in printed books; in television film and drama things are rather better). Nevertheless, since the later fifties – since the coming-of-age of working-class offspring able to benefit from the results of the 1944 Education Act – the lives of the majority have at last been able to find outstanding imaginative interpreters, especially Sillitoe, David Storey, and Barry Hines.[11] The catch is that a writer's habits, the company he keeps and where he lives, are likely to distance him from his roots and move him into the milieux of the middle and upper-middle class (Census Class II, professional and managerial). This in turn can become the writer's subject but this depends on his or her adaptability. Lawrence, for example, was supremely quick at seizing on the essentials of an alien way of life – what would-be militant critics used to call 'betraying his class'. The examples of Hines and Storey are instructive in another way. Hines has worked steadily in veins known to him from his youth in Barnsley, in the West Riding, from his vision of how an undersized lad from a one-parent family could fulfil himself in his relationship with animals to his most recent novels about young people and women struggling to make a living in a country ridden by slump. For Hines, it *is* a matter of being loyal to a class: he sees it as political work to present the dilemmas and qualities of the unprivileged. Storey is much less political; his interests are more inward and psychological. Yet even he is more strictly focussed on his old

11See my 'Sillitoe and the Roots of Anger', in David Craig, *The Real Foundations* (London, Chatto and Windus, 1973), pp. 270–1, 277–9.

class – the coalfield workers and their families in the Wakefield area – than is Sillitoe. As recently as *Saville* (1976) Storey was still moved to spend the most detailed attention on the people from the little houses, who bike or bus to work underground – the milieu also of Hines's television plays and novel *The Price of Coal* (1977, 1979). Yet because a miner's child can climb the schooling ladder to a clean and 'respectable' job, Storey has equally shown the precise circumstances, and the strains, of this process, in the later parts of *Saville* and in *Pasmore* (1972). Sillitoe has his own version of this tendency to move out and away; as we have seen, it is never by that usual ladder of GCE passes, further education, and a white-collar job, nor by that other usual ladder or bridge, emigration (unless Frank Dawley's time in Algeria fighting for the FLN counts as that). Arthur Seaton, Isaac Starbuck, Ken the Chiker itch to take off (but never do) through a sheer chafing at the programmed life. No social path appears to open out before them. The most ambitious and sustained break-out, Frank Dawley's in the 'Bill Posters' trilogy, is purely lonely: he grafts a solidarity with the oppressed people of Algeria onto his inner escapism: 'You worked with those at the bottom in order to be reborn.'[12]

This contrast between Sillitoe and the others applies also to his view of the old home community. For Hines, it is simply there: his unblinking naturalism presents the life of the housing estates and the working men's clubs as just a mixture like any other, although we can infer a cutting-edge of solidarity with the workers from the advantage given to the anti-Royal wit of the miners in *The Price of Coal* and the undeceived dourness with which George Purse looks after his gentleman at the grouse shoot in *The Gamekeeper* (1975). For Storey the old home community is a milieu in which people (miners and their wives) have settled for half, in which they have, often literally, lain down under cramped and mean conditions and to some extent lost the power of living fully as a result.[13]

By contrast, Sillitoe has a much heartier relish and a more settled appreciativeness for the ordinary urban way of life than Hines or Storey. He also turns against it more bitterly. These 'incompatible' attitudes must now be looked into more closely.

Sillitoe's appreciation for the big Midland city in all its sprawl and shabbiness comes out at its purest in the well-being that all kinds of characters repeatedly feel when they are at home in it, for example Arthur Seaton just before being beaten up by Jack's soldier mates:

> His footsteps led between trade-marked houses, two up and two down, with digital chimneys like pigs' tits on the rooftops sending up heat and smoke into the cold trough of a windy sky. . . . Winter was an easy time for him to hide his secrets, for each dark street patted his shoulder and

[12]Alan Sillitoe, *A Tree on Fire* (London, W.H. Allen, 1979), p. 151.
[13]See David Craig, 'David Storey's Vision of the Working Class', in Douglas Jefferson and Graham Martin, eds., *The Uses of Fiction* (Milton Keynes, The Open University Press, 1982), pp. 126–9, 135–7.

became a friend, and the gaseous eye of each lamp glowed unwinking as he passed. Houses lay in rows and ranks, a measure of safety in such numbers, and those within were snug and grateful fugitives from the broad track of bleak winds that brought rain from the Derbyshire mountains and snow from the Lincolnshire Wolds.[14]

In the most basic way the city is a shelter against the elements, and though Arthur's well-being here is inseparable from his sexual contentment, the environment is still crucial to his state of mind, as it is towards the end when the summer routine of fishing along the nearby canal bodies forth his ease in the coming marriage with Doreen:

> Another solitary man was fishing further along the canal, but Arthur knew that they would leave each other in peace, would not even call out greetings. No one bothered you: you were a hunter, a dreamer, your own boss, away from it all for a few hours on any day that the weather did not throw down its rain. Like the corporal in the army who said it was marvellous the things you thought about as you sat on the lavatory.[15]

In such places we feel – and it is a very rare feeling to get from literature – that the main protagonist can at the same time be both himself and part of the urban social norm. He doesn't necessarily have to separate himself from the mundane and average to be himself, to be fulfilled. Almost the opposite is true of all the other protagonists in this line of writing, from Paul Morel in *Sons and Lovers* to Pasmore and Saville, and Billy Casper in Hines's *A Kestrel for a Knave*.

This ability to be at ease in the city is not simplistic or sentimental on Sillitoe's part. In a fine early story, 'The Fishing-boat Picture', the postman is presented throughout as comfortable in a dull way, not much bothered when his wife walks out on him, phlegmatically willing to welcome her back for weekly evening visits when her lover has died, and this is figured in the calm townscape mid-way through the story:

> I was at home, smoking my pipe in the backyard at the fag-end of an autumn day. The sky was a clear yellow, going green above the house-tops and wireless aerials. Chimneys were just beginning to send out evening smoke, and most of the factory motors had been switched off. The noise of kids scooting around lamp-posts and the barking of dogs came from what sounded a long way off.[16]

But Sillitoe knows the limitations of this readiness to make do, and when the postman has not quite been able to bring himself to invite her back, he

[14]Sillitoe, *Saturday Night*, p. 163.
[15]*Op. cit.*, p. 210.
[16]'The Fishing-boat Picture', in Alan Sillitoe, *The Loneliness of the Long-distance Runner* (London, W.H. Allen, 1959), p. 85.

senses his mistake and is left realizing (after her accidental early death) that he has failed:

> I began to believe there was no point in my life – became even too far gone to turn religious or go on the booze. Why had I lived? I wondered. I can't see anything for it. . . .
> I was born dead, I keep telling myself. Everybody's dead, I answer. So they are, I maintain, but then most of them never know it like I'm beginning to do. . . . Yes, I cry, but neither of us *did anything about it*, and that's the trouble.[17]

Sillitoe's people are workers to the core – not token or courtesy workers or abstract human natures with a few proletarian trimmings. They can at times feel their work to be part of themselves, as in a natural moment like this from 'Before Snow Comes':

> He would get clean steel nails and set out those laths and offshoot wasted planks from the trunks of great trees that he got cheap because one of his mates worked there, and brush off the sawdust lovingly from each one, feeling it collect like the wooden gold-dust of life in the palm of his hands and sift between the broad flesh of his lower fingers.[18]

Here Mark is working for himself, or for Jean (it is her garden), but his feeling for materials and processes springs from his whole working life and it is a feeling which in places grows outwards to the extent of making us feel that a person can be at home in a factory – can overcome the alienating effects of divided labour and distant management. At times this seems willed – done more to enforce a doctrine than to express something the author knows and is sure of from the bottom of himself, as when Frank argues with Myra in *The Death of William Posters*: ' "All I believe in is houses and factories, food and power-stations, bridges and coalmines and death, turning millions of things out on a machine that people can use, people who also turn out millions of things that other people can use. It's no use harping back to poaching rights and cottage industries." '[19] Is this not too flatly asserted as speech, too void of character or idiom? The same stiffness comes over the style when Frank, in the Algerian desert, likens his belonging to the freedom fighters' war-machine to his first experience of turning a metal part to the specifications on a blueprint, or when Brian at the end of *Key to the Door* looks forward to working in the same engineering shop as his dad and going to union meetings in the evening.[20] The test is in the quality of the language, and in this respect the long passage presenting the start of Arthur's week in the bicycle factory seems to me faultless:

[17]*Op. cit.*, pp. 94, 99.
[18]Sillitoe, *Men Women and Children*, p. 67.
[19]Sillitoe, *William Posters*, p. 259.
[20]Sillitoe, *Tree on Fire*, p. 192; *Key to the Door*, pp. 444–5.

Arthur reached his capstan lathe and took off his jacket, hanging it on a nearby nail so that he could keep an eye on his belongings. He pressed the starter button, and his motor came to life with a gentle thump. Looking around, it did not seem, despite the infernal noise of hurrying machinery, that anyone was working with particular speed. He smiled to himself and picked up a glittering steel cylinder from the top box of a pile beside him, and fixed it into the spindle. He jettisoned his cigarette into the sud-pan, drew back the capstan, and swung the turret into its broadest drill. Two minutes passed while he contemplated the precise position of tools and cylinder; finally he spat onto both hands and rubbed them together, then switched on the sud-tap from the movable brass pipe, pressed a button that set the spindle running, and ran in the drill to a neat chamfer. Monday morning had lost its terror.[21]

This is the first passage I know of in our literature (nearly two centuries after the first power-loom was patented!) which evokes a factory-worker's experiences from the inside with the finesse that writers have given to all the others in the human range. The emotion suggested in the course of a very practical or technical passage is pleasure in the way things are and in being adept at them. The passage persuades me that a lively and feeling person can find that his own prowess or physical–mental needs are satisfied, at least for a time, by that industrial job. For five or six generations, since the start of the industrial revolution, our writers had figured the factory as Hell.[22] And certainly the full-fledged forms of mass production, on the moving assembly-line, make up a fairly monstrous system; the experience many Ford car workers have of it is summed up in sentences like 'The line here is made for morons' or 'Wind me up at 8 a.m and that's that.'[23] But there are jobs and jobs within the factory. 'The factory' is no more to be stereotyped, as though it was all one and the same, than are 'the home' or 'marriage' It is a vast theatre of the most various human skills and experiences. To do it justice we need, not a single black or blank stereotype (Hell), but a complicated picture rich in evidence from the grassroots.

Sillitoe is equivocal about these roots and tends to deny their relevance to his work. In an introduction he wrote for an edition of *Saturday Night and Sunday Morning* he refers to the 'so-called ''working-class'' ' and goes on to say:

The greatest inaccuracy was ever to call the book a 'working-class novel' for it is really nothing of the sort. It is simply a novel, and the label given it by most reviewers at the time it came out, even the intelligent ones who should have known better, was simply a way of

---

[21]Sillitoe, *Saturday Night*, pp. 28–9.
[22]See David Craig, 'Images of Factory Life', *Gulliver II* II (1977), pp. 100–1; Craig, 'The Crowd in Dickens', in Robert Giddings, ed., *The Changing World of Charles Dickens* (London, Vision Press, 1983), p. 87.
[23]Huw Beynon, *Working for Ford* (London, Allen Lane / Penguin Education, 1973), pp. 114, 119.

categorizing a piece of work they weren't capable of assessing from their narrow class standpoint.[24]

Partly this is the resentment of a young writer at the patronage of people surprised that a novelist could spring from a line of factory workers. But only two years ago he could still write:

> I was amused when reviewers and journalists referred to me as a 'working-class' novelist. In spite of the stage on which I set many of my novels and stories I had ceased to be connected to that part of life from the moment I enlisted in the RAF. Before that time I hadn't heard the phrase, and wouldn't have known what it meant. Then when I became a writer I simply did what any other novelist does, which is to use the first 18 years of his or her life in order to begin writing novels and stories.[25]

To this, I believe, we have to answer 'Never trust the artist. Trust the tale', and the tale of Sillitoe's worth trusting above any other I take to be 'The Good Women'. It was first published in the *Daily Worker* from 26 May to 2 June 1962 and then (with significant small softenings of wording) in *The Ragman's Daughter*. One of its many strengths is that it centres on a character quite distinct from the author – an ordinary working-class mother – whereas in much of his fiction it is only the man, the impatient, overweening, anarchic man, who is fully created and the other characters are a foil to him. Liza Atkin is a woman learning to be militant. Her first experience shaped by politics comes over to her as purely personal: her elder son is killed in the Korean war by an American plane spreading napalm meant for the Communist lines near by. Her dogged sanity shows in her refusal to be funereal about him: 'Liza came down the street next day with a loaf of bread in her hand, biting a piece off now and again. . . . Months later Liza was walking along a lane near Wollaton, and remembered how, at the beginning of the war, Harry and Alf had been evacuated to Workshop. Harry had been sick all the way there on the bus, and she laughed now to think about it.' But she faces her pain squarely: 'Korea was a world, a word, as far off now as somebody else's dream, that had killed Harry, called him up and bombed him to ashes for no good reason, like when you have too many kittens you dunk some in a copper. It wasn't necessary, it was wrong, the bad thing to do.' When it thunders, she projects her rage into the storm: 'I don't know who to blame, she thought, but go on, rip and claw the effing world to pieces. Tear up that bleddy town, sling it to hell.'

Again the story is rare in Sillitoe's work in that Liza finds an outlet for her personal anguish: it transmutes into militancy. When she goes to work in

[24]Alan Sillitoe, *Saturday Night and Sunday Morning*, ed. David Craig (London, Longman, 1968), pp. viii, xii.
[25]Alan Sillitoe, 'Writing and Publishing', *London Review of Books* (1–14 April 1982).

the bike factory, she shows her independence by refusing to be a soft touch when a shop steward assumes he can recruit her for the union without even a minute's explanation, but when a strike is called against being put on short time, she exults in it because 'it was a way of doing damage to those who bossed the world about' – and because the best rank-and-file speaker at the meeting and the march reminds her of her dead son.

He makes two speeches, and they are crucial. Unlike any other political speeches in fiction (most notably the red-dawn rhetoric in Upton Sinclair's *The Jungle*), they are very well written, whether as trenchant expressions of a viewpoint or as dramatic imitations of public speaking in a vernacular:

> 'Well, they can give us that we want in this dispute (and they will, make no mistakes about it) and they can give us a raise when we force the boggers to it, but as far as I'm concerned, it'll be like them smallpox jabs I had. It wain't take. It's not a raise here and a bit of an improvement there that we want – none of it'll take. It's a whole bloody change' – his wide-apart fists gave a slow forceful turning motion as if at the wheel of some great ship and making a violent alteration in its course – 'a turnover from top to bottom. . . .'

As the main narrative comes to an end, the prose balances wonderfully between evoking this particular woman's thoughts and a slightly more impersonal vision which gives us, more convincingly and clearly than anything else I know in the literature of our time, a definition of the impasse, the locked-up potential, which exists in our world:

> 'I knew we'd get what we wanted,' Liza said, exulting before those along the bench at how she had marched downtown with 2,000 men, as if inviting them to tease and remind her of it of often as they liked. Yet she felt that the strike had never really ended, that such a downing of tools meant little because instead of coming back to work they should have stayed out solid and gone on from there.
>
> Something other than the mere petty end of an industrial dispute lay beyond them, the half-felt, intangible presence of an abyss that needed crossing for everything to be settled once and for all. They had had enough, but Liza, passing the thousands of components through her gauges at the bench, recalled the tall young man speaking on the first day of the walk-out, and knew that he and many others scattered through the factory also considered that something else was in front of them, a great space of freedom and change not too far beyond the feet and eyes.[26]

To write so well about 'that part of life', you cannot have 'ceased to be connected' with it. Your line through to it must be clear and many-fibred,

[26]Quoted from both versions: *Daily Worker* (26 May–2 June); Alan Sillitoe, *The Ragman's Daughter* (London, W.H. Allen, 1963), pp. 169–72, 182, 185–6.

even though it now consists of memories, language-habits, and, presumably, surviving family relationships, and not any longer of actual membership. Sillitoe's own wisest thoughts on the class question, at the level of explicit comment, occur in the Author's Note to *Men Women and Children* where he writes:

> I again use Nottingham and its county as my stage, though it is unnecessary to point out that the breadth of activity, of movement and suffering, is as intense and deep when undergone by the people on this stage as on any other. . . . emotions have to be delineated in the minds of people who are not usually prone to describing them. The same emotions and feelings are of course felt by them as by more voluble and literate people. . . . [They] have the same sufferings as kings and queens, but their daily problems are more fundamental and tormenting.[27]

He has also said that the great problem for a writer starting out is 'to remain true to what he has'[28] and on the evidence of his work we have to say that what he has is an undying imaginative participation in the lives of the people he lived amongst for his first 19 years. It is because these were working-class people that it is necessary, and not misleading, to call him a working-class writer.

In *Men Women and Children* Sillitoe also says that 'Those complicated people who are less down to earth are in many ways easier to describe, or at least no more difficult.' His own practice suggests that for him this is actually not so. I question whether he has ever successfully created a character from the middle or upper-middle class. Yet his later novels have, inevitably, taken him in that direction. At the same time he has been trying out veins of boisterous, not to say frantic, picaresque. The result is this kind of image of artists, intellectuals, media people, and other types from 'Home Counties, Census Class II':

> One crumby pub was bunged up to the gills, but along the bar was a face I'd seen before. . . . He was a tall man, dressed in a high-necked sweater and an expensive tweed jacket, the sort of casual gear that must have cost far more than a good suit. His face was, I suppose, sensitive because of the thick lips, putty skin, and pale eyes. He wore a hat, but in spite of this I was struck by the length of his face and head, which did not however make him as ugly as it should have done. . . . it was sharp-eyed June who told me he was a writer by the name of Gilbert Blaskin.

This writer's conversation consists exclusively of far-fetched drivel, monologues elaborating the plot of his 'latest novel' and the like, and after one such sequence the hero (a refugee from the Midland working class, of

[27]Sillitoe, *Men Women and Children*, p. 10.
[28]Special Correspondent, 'Alan Sillitoe', *The Times* (6 February 1964).

course) puts him down as follows: 'I got up and put the coffee back on the stove, while he chewed the fat of his insane liver that lived off the fat of the land. I wished I'd been working in a factory so that I could have told him to belt up and get some real work done.'[29]

My criticism of this kind of thing is that it is too approximate and the authorial prompting too browbeating. Sillitoe doesn't have the satirist's gift of letting us see the precise features of the original just under the deformities of the cartoon. Whenever he touches at all on the lives of the white-collared, he is driven to violent caricature. This disfigures the whole part of the 'Bill Posters' trilogy which is set in England, particularly amongst the family of Albert Handley, the Great Painter, who stands for anarchic creativity. His wife's haranguing of a visiting Sunday-paper journalist is typical:

> 'There are some people to whom being an out-and-out bastard gives strength. Oh, I don't mean the weedy or puffy sort who never have the strength to be real bastards anyway, like you. But I mean the man who, not strong in the beginning, like Albert, soon finds himself becoming so when he gets money, and the *urge to be a swine gets into his blood.*'[30]

The context leaves us in no doubt that the Handleys embody Life, as against the half-life of almost everybody else, and the author tries to equip them with radical credentials which will complete their image as the last word in fearless authentic living. None of this has the least reality: Handley's eldest son, Richard (one of seven children), is at one point supposed to be sending the plans of 'secret bases' to Moscow rolled in a bundle of *New Statesman*s.[31] Satirist's licence? Yet, throughout, the Handleys triumph much too easily for us to feel that they are in any way placed or qualified by their creator. The feeling is that they embody what he has now come to be himself – a part of privileged, successful England yet still hankering to defy and discredit it.

The lesson would seem to be that if you are to do so, you must at least have become, imaginatively, master of the middle-class milieux in which you now find yourself. One touchstone for this is Storey: as we have seen, he has gone on cleaving more closely to his old class than has Sillitoe, yet when he has needed to present the owners, managers, and rulers, his touch has been unerring. Consider the subtlety with which the manipulations of Weaver, the works owner and rugby club director in *This Sporting Life*, are evoked by physical and dramatic means.[32] Or think of the truly sinister power (created by terse, low-key writing from which violent moments erupt) of those twin figures, Helen's husband in *Pasmore* and Newman in *A Temporary Life* (1973). Both are 'self-made men' (counterparts of Claud

[29]Alan Sillitoe, *A Start in Life* (London, W.H. Allen, 1970), pp. 173, 184.
[30]Sillitoe, *Tree on Fire*, p. 27.
[31]*Op. cit.*, p. 41.
[32]See Craig, 'Hear Them Talking To You', in *The Real Foundations*, pp. 266–8.

Moggerhanger in *A Start in Life*): without the least strain or excess Storey is able to establish them as black presences below the surface of the business world – representatives of those club-owners and property dealers who have taken recently to funding the British fascist parties, setting up connections with the Mafia-based drug trade, and so on.

The most complete touchstone is Lawrence – from the same part of England as Sillitoe, making the same moves as his career blossomed, earning the same equivocal standing in his old community. Lawrence shows a valuable self-knowledge in the letter where he remarks on one of his own working-class qualities, as he sees it, a 'jeering and purpleism', which are also common in Sillitoe but given free rein, not understood self-critically. Both men curse straitlaced, habit-bound England in very similar terms so far as explicit comment goes. But here the resemblance ends. Lawrence feels to be as at home when he is characterizing the 'well-bred' intellectuals, mine-owners, and hostesses in *Women in Love*, for example, as he is when he is evoking the shabby-genteel life of Ursula and Gudrun's parents. Again, when he moves amongst the London smart set and their horse-riding county friends in *St Mawr*, he is able to dramatize them satirically while not deforming or diminishing their reality as persons; he writes about this milieu with decisive sardonic criticism but not with animus (Leavis's valuable distinction[33]). For example, with that caricature of Gilbert Blaskin in *A Start in Life* compare this image of Rico, the dilettante painter son of an Australian baronet, being got at by his dissatisfied young wife ('moderately rich . . . Louisiana family, moved down to Texas'):

'Rico dear, you must get a horse.'
The tone was soft and southern and drawling, but the overtone had a decisive finality. In vain Rico squirmed – he had a way of writhing and squirming which perhaps he had caught at Oxford. In vain he protested that he couldn't ride, and that he didn't care for riding. He got quite angry, and his handsome arched nose tilted and his upper lip lifted from his teeth, like a dog that is going to bite. Yet daren't quite bite.
And that was Rico. He daren't quite bite. Not that he was really afraid of the others. He was afraid of himself, once he let himself go. He might rip up in an eruption of life-long anger all this pretty-pretty picture of a charming young wife and a delightful little home and a fascinating success as a painter of fashionable, and at the same time 'great', portraits: with colour, wonderful colour, and at the same time, form, marvellous form. He had composed this little *tableau vivant* with great effort. He didn't want to erupt like some suddenly wicked horse. . . .[34]

[33]F.R. Leavis, *D.H. Lawrence: Novelist* (London, Chatto and Windus, 1955), p. 276.
[34]'St Mawr', in *The Tales of D.H. Lawrence* (London, Heinemann, 1934), pp. 561–2.

Lawrence is able to conceive of such a person psychologically even while he places him satirically as a social being. For Sillitoe, people from outside his old home community are nearly always butts. And this connects with the spasms of aggression when he tries to get Them in his sights – his gun-sights.[35] In spite of such violent squaring-up, and the constant use of 'Communism' like an incantation (no main character is ever a Communist but the cousins and uncles, off-stage, often are), it is very rare for Sillitoe to present a substantial conflict between Us and Them. (The clearly articulated industrial dispute in 'The Good Women' is an exception, as is the Algeria section of the Frank Dawley trilogy). The more rebellious of the Us people are therefore left to fulminate in a kind of vacuum – to pedal round and round in the cycles of their rage without their energy being geared to anything much outside themselves. And Sillitoe seems not to know this clearly enough, which gives rise to the wild swipes at the white-collared and also to a great deal of overblown phrase-making, mixed metaphors, a diarrhoea of adjectives: as Storey puts it in that important early review, 'whenever passion fails, it's the words themselves that unsuccessfully he tries to whip along'.

The final thoughts of that review remain hard to dissent from, even though Sillitoe has produced another 20 years' work since then:

> Continually it's suggested that society alone inspires rebellion without any awareness that we are condemned to find in society very much of what we wish to find there. . . . If one is increasingly exasperated by Sillitoe's beating at those out there rather than at the thing inside it is because his particular pain – the agony that runs like an underground torrent through *Saturday Night and Sunday Morning* – is one that is so important and yet one that is rapidly being sentimentalised. He has shown us his gesture, and we've seen it; now let us hear the cry within.[36]

My own review of *A Start in Life* 14 years ago arrived at a kindred point when it said that Sillitoe's talent 'may fray itself out for good unless he now makes himself become less headlong in his output, perhaps by holding back from easy identification with the rogue male and by weighing up more thoughtfully what it is that he has against our present way of life.'[37] I still hope that he may try to explore the deeper, more psychological levels of experience, bosses' as well as workers', in the industrial community with the intensity that he has been so good at focussing on its more outward incidents and characters.

---

[35]Sillitoe, *Saturday Night*, pp. 134–5; *The Loneliness of the Long-distance Runner*, p. 33; *William Posters*, p. 315: 'The kick at his shoulder was the joy of life.'
[36]Storey, 'Which revolution?'.
[37]*The Times Literary Supplement* (14 September 1970).

Note

I list below books which include treatments of the working class by the principal authors discussed in the body of my article.

Patrick MacGill, *Children of the Dead End* (Dingle, Co. Kerry, Brandon Books, 1982; first published London, Herbert Jenkins, 1914).

Patrick MacGill, *Moleskin Joe* (London, Caliban Books, 1983; first published London, Herbert Jenkins, 1923).

Patrick MacGill, *The Rat-Pit* (Dingle, Co. Kerry, Brandon Books, 1982; first published London, Herbert Jenkins, 1915).

Michael McLaverty, *Call My Brother Back* (Swords, Co. Dublin, Poolbeg Press, 1979; first published London, Jonathan Cape, 1939).

Michael McLaverty, *Lost Fields* (Swords, Co. Dublin, Poolbeg Press, 1980; first published London, Longman, 1942).

Frank O'Connor (pseud. of Michael O'Donovan), *Collected Stories* (New York, Knopf, 1981).

Frank O'Connor, *Collection Three* (London, Macmillan, 1969).

Frank O'Connor, *Collection Two* (London, Macmillan, 1964).

Frank O'Connor, *The Cornet Player Who Betrayed Ireland and Other Stories* (Swords, Co. Dublin, Poolbeg Press, 1981).

Frank O'Connor, *An Only Child* (London, Macmillan; Knopf, New York, 1961).

Frank O'Connor, *The Saint and Mary Kate* (London, Macmillan, 1932).

Frank O'Connor, *The Stories of Frank O'Connor* (London, Hamish Hamilton, 1953).

James Stephens, *The Charwoman's Daughter* (Dublin, Gill and Macmillan, 1972; first published London, Macmillan, 1912).

James Stephens, 'Hunger', in *Desire and Other Stories* (Swords, Co. Dublin, Poolbeg Press, 1981; first published as a booklet under the pseudonym 'James Esse', Dublin, The Candle Press, 1918. Included in *Etched in Moonlight*, London, Macmillan, 1928).

8

The Irish Working Class in Fiction

Ruth Sherry

The concept of Irish working-class writing is not a well-established one. There is scarcely any nineteenth-century Irish fiction which can be said to treat the working classes, apart perhaps from a handful of novels, virtually all written by middle-class women, which deal either with life in urban slums or with conditions in domestic (cottage) industry. These novels are all now forgotten; there was no Irish writer as central as Elizabeth Gaskell or Charles Dickens who took up this subject matter. There was likewise no parallel in Ireland to the writing which, in England, came from the pens of industrial workers themselves, in the wake of the Chartist movement.

In the twentieth century the situation in the two islands becomes somewhat more similar, but is scarcely identical. In both cases one finds middle-class writers who depict working-class life, while in Ireland for the first time writers appear who have their own origins in the working classes, although some of the most prominent of these, such as Sean O'Casey and Brendan Behan, made their major contributions in drama rather than in fiction.

When one thinks of the working class, with the English experience and English fiction as a starting point, one generally thinks of industrial workers and of an urban population, or perhaps a mining community. But any discussion of the Irish working class in fiction is implicitly conditioned by the very different demographic and economic situation of Ireland, where the population is very little urbanized even today. There are only three major centres: Dublin, Belfast and Cork, and of these, only Belfast experienced significant effects of the Industrial Revolution, which was largely confined to the north-eastern part of the island.

In Britain (i.e. the island of Great Britain), the agriculturally based population remained the same, in absolute terms, throughout the nineteenth century, while at the same time cities burgeoned, especially in the north of England, and the population of the whole island increased dramatically. In Ireland, however, rural population declined drastically in the nineteenth century without any corresponding growth in any town but Belfast; in fact the populations of Dublin and Cork also declined in the middle of the century, while the growth of Belfast, although not arrested, slowed down noticeably in the same period. To put it another way, when the Famine of the 1840s led to the depopulation of the rural areas of Ireland, there was insufficient industrial occupation in the towns to absorb the displaced population, and emigration or death resulted.

Another pattern, over a somewhat longer period, is of the centralization and decline of such industry as existed. In many cases a traditional, originally domestic, industry went from being small-scale but widespread to being concentrated in a few urban centres; brewing and woollens are examples. The smaller Irish cities have stagnated and now provide relatively little industrial occupation. Likewise, in contrast to the situation in England, Irish industry did not on the whole move into new areas of heavier industry in the later nineteenth century. With the notable exception of the shipyards in Belfast, Irish industries have remained the older, traditional ones: brewing and distilling, processing of agricultural produce, textiles. Even the well-developed industries have proved highly vulnerable in bad times and in the face of foreign competition. Some, like cotton, which expanded for a time, have now disappeared; others, like the once-prosperous shipbuilding, are continually threatened.

The overall result is that the range of occupations available to those migrating to Irish towns has historically been narrower than that available to similarly situated people in Britain. Service rather than production occupations have provided a greater proportion of the available jobs; there has likewise been a greater predominance of unskilled jobs, notably in construction and transport, where the work is often seasonal. All these by their nature tend to provide less stable employment than the skilled occupations. Thus while English working-class fiction typically focuses on factory workers and miners and their families, these receive comparatively little attention in Irish writing, simply because these occupations are less predominant; mining, for example, is virtually non-existent.

There is no single universally agreed definition of what constitutes the 'working class', but as many of the usual definitions take their starting point in industry, they are relatively less applicable to the Irish situation. Some groups of people, especially those employed in service occupations, therefore seem to fall outside, though culturally, economically and socially they may be in a situation similar to that of industrial workers. In Ireland, domestic servants, in particular, have historically constituted a very large proportion of workers. An additional problem is that most concepts of the working class tend to take as a starting point the occupation of a male head of household. The idea that women do not work, or that their work is not significant for a family's status, is however a middle-class idea. Not only do women, as domestic servants, constitute a central group, they have also provided a very high proportion of the labour in one of the major Irish industries, linen.

All of these circumstances are inevitably reflected in Irish fiction. While there are few Irish parallels to *Sons and Lovers* or *Saturday Night and Sunday Morning*, there are a number of striking works of fiction which in one way or another present the experience of Irish people who are at the lower end of the social and economic scale whose lives, at the same time, are not exclusively rural – perhaps the closest one can come to a satisfactory definition of the Irish working class.

One novel which illustrates the problems of definition at the same time that it points up distinctive and characteristic elements of the Irish experience is a recently re-discovered masterpiece, Patrick MacGill's *Children of the Dead End* (1914).[1] MacGill (1890–1963) was born in Glenties, Co. Donegal; by his own account his novel is largely autobiographical. The central character and narrator is Dermod Flynn, the eldest of a large number of children in a Catholic tenant-farming family. Life at home in Glenmornan is difficult; there is a constant struggle to make up the rent and the 'dues' for the parish priest. Dermod's brother dies because there is no money to pay for the doctor – although there is money to pay the rent. Dermod is sent to the hiring fair in Strabane at the age of 12; then he works on three different Co. Tyrone farms in conditions which range from harsh to benevolent but even at best offer him little scope for self-determination. Growing eager for independence, he leaves a good farm to join a party travelling from Glenmornan to Scotland to harvest potatoes. Women as well as men are part of the harvesting gang; they travel from farm to farm, living and working in appalling conditions, housed worse than animals, liable to every kind of demoralization. After the harvest season Dermod tramps and begs in Scotland until eventually he is taken onto a railroad gang after another man is horribly killed. After more tramping he spends a long period working on the construction of a waterworks in the Highlands where thousands of navvies together lead a distorted and unnatural existence. He begins to write accounts of the life of the construction camp which attract the attention of a London editor, and he works briefly as a journalist in London. He returns to Glasgow to find Norah Ryan, his old sweetheart from Glenmornan; originally destined to become a nun, in Scotland she has been seduced, made pregnant, and abandoned. As the novel ends, she dies.

The obvious question which arises is in what sense this can be called an Irish working-class novel. The first third of it is about agricultural labour, not work in transportation or industry, and only about a quarter of the whole novel is set in Ireland. No one reading only that portion of it set in Ireland would be likely to call it a working-class novel; it would, rather, be labelled a novel about Irish rural life. One might say that it is a working-class novel only insofar as it is British, not Irish.

Yet *Children of the Dead End* reflects a pattern particularly typical for Ireland: landlessness leads to rural destitution, which leads to migration, finally to emigration. *Children of the Dead End* might thus be called a novel about the *creation* of the working class. Much of its emphasis is on displacement and, with that, corresponding changes of values.

Even after his emigration to Scotland, Dermod's standard of identity remains Irish; for a long time he persists in trying to behave 'like a Glenmornan man', and his Glenmornan sweetheart remains his most

[1]*Children of the Dead End* (Brandon, Dingle, Co. Kerry, 1982).

important emotional tie. Yet gradually the values of Donegal are questioned and discarded. Dermod comes to rebel against the idea that he should keep sending his wages to provide for his parents' ever-increasing brood: shouldn't they rather stop having so many children? Dermod also comes to reject both religion and capitalism. As a child he rebelled against a tyrannical teacher, later he stood up to a cruel farmer. Faced with injustice on the railroad he makes a brave, though unsuccessful, attempt to lead a strike. Organized religion is no better; although Jesus was a working man, the churches serve the interests of the propertied classes. Dermod becomes a convinced socialist.

MacGill's novel is particularly powerful in its depiction of work. Almost all of the labour available is physically debilitating, and it is often performed in degrading, sometimes downright dangerous, conditions. MacGill's style is for the most part clear and simple; it is easy to see why he showed promise as a journalist, for his force as a writer depends upon a largely unprejudiced eye and an attention to detail. He is matter-of-fact in his treatment of the moral element in the lives of his labourers: drinking and gambling provide an escape from brutality and emptiness. Fighting in the physical sense becomes a major value, a source of power, identity and pride, although working men direct their physical aggression against each other, not outward toward the oppressor. Although his political convictions are consistent with the picture he presents in his fiction, MacGill's works are not propagandistic and offer no detailed programme for change. The novel is in this way characteristic of most Irish writing about the working classes; there is no significant Irish category of 'socialist fiction' which overlaps with 'working-class fiction', as one finds in England.

Children of the Dead End is weakest in its treatment of Norah Ryan, to whom Dermod responds largely in terms of sentimental clichés. He 'loves' her but responds to her 'purity' rather than acknowledging that she is sexually desirable. As a fallen woman – soon disencumbered of her son, who dies in early childhood – she is thus simultaneously virgin and whore, and the conventionality of her death sounds a false note in a novel otherwise so directly observed and frankly presented. It is therefore particularly striking that in 1915, several months after *Children of the Dead End*, MacGill published another novel, *The Rat-Pit*, which interlocks with *Children of the Dead End* and follows Norah through the same period of time as that covered by the first novel.[2] *The Rat-Pit* is told in the third person, and thus retains a certain distance in its treatment of Norah but, although it is not entirely devoid of convention and sentimentality, this novel is much more frank and realistic than the first in its treatment of Norah's experiences, and it is particularly notable for its accounts of the lives of women of the labouring class. In Glenmornan the women knit stockings for as long as 16 hours a day, earning a penny-farthing for the product of these hours of labour; the tiny recompense is nevertheless crucial for the family's income. In Glasgow women make shirts or jackets at

[2]*The Rat-Pit* (Brandon, Dingle, Co. Kerry, 1982).

home under conditions that are no better; they must sew 20 hours a day just to maintain existence. Health is inevitably affected, but there is no time to be ill. Children are neglected, however much loved, and prostitution is deliberately chosen as providing the only realistic alternative to starvation.

Characters from these two novels reappear in some of MacGill's later work, but these first two parallel novels are striking because of the implication that the experience of women should be given equal weight to that of men if the whole truth is to be told.

Insofar as Donegal was part of the old nine-county province of Ulster, MacGill was an Ulster writer, but his characters do not contemplate migrating to Belfast in search of employment. For people from western Ulster, the boat from Derry to Glasgow provided the obvious route of migration. Nevertheless, many Ulster people did make the move to Belfast, although they were likely to come from Antrim, Armagh or Down rather than from the more distant counties. Not surprisingly, Ulster has produced more working-class writers than any other part of Ireland, although few of their names are well-known even elsewhere in the country. One of the better-known is Michael McLaverty (1907–   ), who was one of the migrants from the countryside. He was brought to Belfast as a child from an island off the Antrim coast and his first novel, *Call My Brother Back* (1939),[3] follows a child who has a similar experience, growing up in a working-class district of the city at about the time of the First World War. In another novel, *Lost Fields* (1942),[4] he treats a later generation. This novel follows the fortunes of a large Catholic family in Belfast over the course of about a year and a half, apparently in the 1930s, and provides a rich but muted account of the details of Belfast working-class life in that period.

The father, Johnny, is a first-generation migrant from the country who has left his mother's home because it could not provide support for a family. At first he found work in a cotton mill, but the mill closed; when the novel opens, he is trying to make a living with his hand-cart as a carrier. Later, when even this work becomes hard to find, Johnny resorts to trading, 'buying a basket of odd delf in Smithfield, hawking it round the entries and exchanging a mug or a bowl for rags or scrap iron'.[5] The entrepreneur is not included in most definitions of the working class, but *Lost Fields* clearly demonstrates that buying and selling is not an activity confined to the *petit bourgeoisie*: a bottle-and-rag man who appears in the novel is closer to destitution than any of his customers. Early in the century, Charles Booth noted that an increase in the trading component of the Irish economy did not by any means imply that more goods were being produced or that there was more money around to purchase them; rather, the situation pointed to the lack of other available occupations.[6] Although of

[3]*Call My Brother Back* (Poolbeg Press, Swords, Co. Dublin, 1979).
[4]*Lost Fields* (Poolbeg Press, Swords, Co. Dublin, 1980).
[5]*Op. cit.*, p. 111.
[6]Charles Booth, 'The Economic Distribution of Population', in Department of Agriculture

course a minority of small traders could prove fortunate and move upward in the social scale, Johnny's trade from his cart scarcely removed him from the ranks of the working classes; if anything, it pushes him further downward on the social scale.

Johnny's family includes his wife; a grown but unemployed son, Hugh; a grown daughter, Mary, who wants to be a nun; two younger sons, three small daughters, and a baby boy. All live in a small house in 'River Street'; the river, changing with the seasons, provides a backdrop and links the life of the family, however, tenuously, with the natural world. A greyhound and a lark kept in a cage are further reminders of another kind of life.

Johnny's family home, a small Co. Antrim farm, plays a major role in the novel as a contrast to the city. When one son, Peter, falls foul of his parents, he steals a bicycle to ride the 30 miles to his grandmother who will, he knows, take him in, feed him, warm him and sympathize with him. When times become particularly hard for the family in Belfast, the grandmother, with her pension, becomes the only possibility of economic survival for them. Persuaded by a sense of duty, she leaves her cottage to join the throng in the tiny house in the city, but over a period of several months she weakens and dies, destroyed, as everyone recognizes, by the break with the countryside, for which she has never ceased to long.

Throughout the novel, the family's fortunes waver. Johnny finds it less and less possible to earn a living. Peter is put into reform school, Hugh is imprisoned for resisting bailiffs who come to evict the family. Escape routes are unreliable: Mary fulfils her only desire when she enters a convent, but she is sent home again because her health is too frail to sustain the life. Yet even the misfortunes sometimes have a beneficial side: Peter is persecuted in reform school, but he is fed, as Hugh is in prison. Both emerge stouter, Peter better clothed as well. Although Hugh is punished for his rebellion, he does succeed in preventing the eviction. The novel unemphatically establishes the cohesion of the family, but shows that its survival exacts a price. The grandmother's move to the city not only leads to her death, it also causes her estrangement from Hugh, who wants to get married and has no place to bring his bride but the room now occupied by his grandmother.

The conclusion of the novel is entirely coherent but also surprising because it seems historically atypical. Unable to find work in the city, Johnny by degrees moves back to his mother's tiny farm in the country. Whereas at one time the city offered better prospects for keeping a family than a three-acre holding, as times become worse this no longer holds true, especially once the oldest children are able to support themselves, Hugh labouring in a brickyard, Mary gone into domestic service. Johnny says, 'We haven't much. . . . We'll always be living from hand to mouth – yet we'll not starve. We've good firing and a free house.'[7] Landholding, for all its vicissitudes, offers a slightly larger measure of economic security than

and Technical Instruction for Ireland, *Ireland: Industrial and Agricultural* (Dublin, Browne and Nolan, 1902), p. 68.
[7]*Lost Fields*, p. 201.

the dead-end of carting and trading. This return to the farm leaves Hugh and his young wife in sole possession of the Belfast house, the core of a new Belfast working-class family.

Lost Fields has affinities with *Children of the Dead End* and *The Rat-Pit* in the sense that life in the 'home place' remains a standard of value and a source of identity long after it has been left behind. This sense of the loss that goes with displacement is a persistent one in Irish life; in recent years in Dublin, for example, loaded coaches have departed every weekend to take young city workers back to their homes 'down the country' where they could find no work. *Lost Fields* however presents a considerably more idyllic picture of country life – for all its acknowledged hardships – than MacGill's works do. Likewise, although it scarcely creates a cosy picture of Belfast working-class life, McLaverty's novel does recognize some positive elements in it. The solidarity of neighbours becomes vital in a time of crisis such as the eviction, and a crowded neighbourhood provides interest and companionship. While there is deprivation, there is also variety, as is shown by set-pieces such as a description of an open-air market and of children playing the traditional 'Queen o' May' game. Small pleasures are not always out of reach: sweets, an occasional glass of porter, a balloon.

McLaverty's great gift is for a careful but selective recounting of the details of everyday life. His style is deceptively unpretentious but unfailingly lucid. The plot is handled lightly; shifts of point-of-view are frequent but unemphatic, and there is no attempt to follow all of the characters in equal detail throughout the novel; although Peter's first days at reform school are treated in detail, for most of his period of detention he is almost forgotten, while the narrative focuses on its main subject, the changes taking place at home.

McLaverty provides little authorial comment or profound psychological analysis, though he frequently follows a character's train of thought and feeling. For the most part his characters' motivations are what they appear to be: no socio-psychological analysis is given of Peter's stealing, and one is left to conclude that he steals for the obvious reason that otherwise he can't get the very ordinary things he wants. Hugh's antagonism toward his grandmother has little to do with her personally, everything to do with a normal young man's desire for a wife and a home.

Nor is McLaverty a politically militant writer, although he records clearly a sense of the injustice of the existing order of things, including an awareness that Johnny's family is not the worst off in Belfast:

> 'I'm thinking we're not as badly off as some people. I saw two old women, as old as myself, out gathering cinders, and this Ash Wednesday morning. Surely to the good God them poor women don't need to be rubbed with ashes to be cleansed of their sins. . . . I'm telling you . . . we'll get a quare judgment on the Last Day. There's something wrong and wicked in a world where old women are out picking cinders on an Ash Wednesday morning.'[8]

[8]*Op. cit.*, p. 102.

McLaverty's works (many of which are about the country, not the city) on the whole reflect a conviction of the basic decency of most people. Although there is no accounting for differences in temper and personality, those who fail are generally weak rather than corrupt. In *Lost Fields*, one is struck by the careful care the family provides for the old grandmother; their solicitude is by no means merely a matter of preserving their main source of income. She, in her turn, dies because she recognizes a duty toward them, however painful she finds it to carry out. Hugh's young wife waits uncomplainingly until they can marry, cheerfully cares for her young sisters- and brothers-in-law, and misses them all when they leave. Friction between the women is almost unknown. Johnny and Hugh are sober, earnest, hard-working – as unlike, for example, the self-indulgent, bullying, indolent Captain Boyle of *Juno and the Paycock* as can be imagined. But these virtues are not sentimentalized, nor indeed underlined in any way; they are presented matter-of-factly, as part of the normal emotional furniture of everyday life. In the end, the family, despite its sufferings and losses, remains a unit, and is in a sense rewarded for its endurance by a return to the equivocal paradise of the lost fields.

If MacGill's and McLaverty's novels each present certain problems of definition when one labels them 'working-class novels', the Dublin author James Stephens (?1882–1950) presents quite a different set of problems. It is difficult to be precise about whether he himself was working class in origin because the circumstances of his parentage, birth and childhood remain a mystery. It seems probable, although not certain, that from the age of four he was raised in the Meath Protestant Industrial School for Boys, an institution which housed quite young boys who had somehow caught the attention of the law; there they were trained to be skilled manual workers or clerks, on the edge between working class and lower middle class. If Stephens was in fact placed in this school, it was for begging – which in itself would suggest either that he was homeless or that his parents could not care for him properly.

As a writer Stephens is usually thought of as a poet and fantasist, not a realist, and most of his writings which are not sheer fantasy are psychological studies with middle-class settings. Before establishing himself as a writer, Stephens worked as a clerk. However, some of his earliest poems deal with injustice and the life of the city streets, and two of his most famous prose works, *The Charwoman's Daughter* (1912) and 'Hunger' (1918),[9] do focus on the working classes. Augustine Martin has said that *The Charwoman's Daughter* is the first novel to deal with the Dublin slums;[10] while this statement may not be strictly accurate, Stephens' is certainly the earliest such novel still read today.

'Hunger' is the only one of Stephens' works that might seem to offer a possible insight into his early life. He observed of it, 'the story is a true one,

---

[9]*The Charwoman's Daughter* (Dublin, Gill and Macmillan, 1972); 'Hunger', in *Desire and Other Stories* (Poolbeg Press, Swords, Co. Dublin, 1980).
[10]Augustine Martin, Introduction to *The Charwoman's Daughter*, p. 4.

and would have killed me but that I got it out of my system this way'.[11] The subject of 'Hunger' is, simply, starvation. A house painter has a steady income only in the summer; when he becomes ill, even that is diminished. He and his wife have three children, and she cannot work because one of them is crippled and requires constant attention. With the advent of the First World War trade contracts dangerously for people whose income is already precarious. One of the children dies of a sickness 'which, whatever it was at the top, was hunger at the bottom'.[12] The father at last goes to Scotland to seek work in a munitions factory but, though he is taken on, he dies of hunger and exposure before he has worked long enough to be paid. At home in Dublin, another child dies before the mother is able to obtain some relief from a charitable benefactor.

The story is told from a point-of-view close to the mother. Although Stephens is especially noted for the lyricism of his prose, the style here is, for him, bare, but there is a submerged rhythm and a savagery which occasionally becomes explicit: 'She was frightened, for one can be arrested for begging. And she was afraid not to beg, for one can die of hunger.'[13]

Although Stephens, a supporter of James Larkin and of Sinn Fein, had strong political convictions, he is not usually thought of as a political writer. More like McLaverty than MacGill, he presents no villains in 'Hunger.' The existing economic and political order seems to be regarded by the characters as inevitable. War does not appear as something which has been chosen by anyone or has any purpose – it merely happens. Yet Stephens leaves no doubts about the injustice of the existing distribution of wealth:

> She followed people with her eyes, sometimes a little way with her feet, saying to herself:
> 'The pockets of that man are full of money; he would rattle if he fell.'

Or:

> 'That man had his breakfast this morning: he is full of food to the chin; he is round and tight and solid and he weighs a ton.'[14]

Poverty precludes resistance, rendering its victims voiceless, politically impotent. 'She did not argue about the matter. . . . If she claimed to possess an opinion it might jeopardize her chance of getting anything.'[15]

The story tends to focus on the internal states of the characters rather

[11]Quoted by Augustine Martin in Introduction to *Desire and Other Stories*, p. 10. Also cited by Patricia McFate, *The Writings of James Stephens: Variations on a Theme of Love* (London, Macmillan, 1979), p. 134. Neither gives a source.
[12]'Hunger', p. 131.
[13]*Op. cit.*, p. 131.
[14]*Op. cit.*, p. 134.
[15]*Op. cit.*, p. 135.

than on the social and economic circumstances which have trapped them, but such details as are given, accurately mirror a typical pattern. The married couple have evidently migrated from the country, as all their relatives are there, too far away to help. The husband, when not working as a house-painter, takes a variety of unskilled jobs of the kind typically available in Dublin: window cleaner, dockworker, coalman, night watchman. The wife, had she been free to go out, would have had no options other than domestic service, sweated labour, and begging.

The Charwoman's Daughter is less bleak, more fanciful, than 'Hunger', but it also engages in more explicit comment on economics and the class system, and is firmly based on the reality that Dublin offers little other employment than domestic service to women – yet there are a great many women for whom work is essential.

Gerd Bjørhovde has pointed out that, although middle-class English women were pioneers in bringing the Industrial Revolution into fiction, English working-class women have themselves produced no fiction.[16] The same is the case in Ireland: there is no Irish Tillie Olsen. One notes in particular the lack of any fiction from the multitude of women workers in the Ulster linen industry; it is a measure of the myriad disadvantages under which working-class women have laboured.

In English working-class fiction, the world presented often seems overwhelmingly masculine, or women, where included, are there largely to provide sexual complications. One can find parallels in some minor Irish writers such as Christy Brown and Lee Dunne, but on the whole there is a surprising impression that Irish men write with considerable understanding of working women, who are accorded a large part in their fiction. Is it merely a coincidence that the author of *Esther Waters* was an Irishman?

One frequently proposed explanation for the relative importance of women in the Irish male imagination rests upon the relatively weak economic postion of the men. Husbands and fathers, dependent upon unskilled or seasonal work, are not necessarily the most stable source of income. Domestic work, performed by women, is badly paid but may provide a steadier income. Even where a man's work is steady, the woman's frequently provides a crucial supplement. These circumstances may have helped to ensure that the economic role of women is not submerged entirely, and that they therefore are accorded a place in the minds and imaginations of the male writers.

Another, and simpler, explanation is that fathers frequently are simply absent. Like the husband in 'Hunger', they have gone 'over the water' to where the work is. One notable expedient, especially in hard times, is the army; Irishmen in their thousands joined the British army in the world wars even in the absence of conscription or in the face of the declared neutrality of the 26 counties. Women whose husbands were on active service were

---

[16]Gerd Bjørhovde, 'Den Britisk Industrialismen og Kvinnen: om Utvikling av et Litteraert Motiv', in *Arbeiderklassekvinner i Litteraturen* (Tromsø, Universitetsforlaget, 1982), p. 67.

paid 'separation money', and were frequently far better off than they ever had been with their husbands at home.

The role of the military in working-class life emerges particularly clearly in the work of Frank O'Connor (1903–66), whose autobiography *An Only Child* provides a classic and unequalled account of working-class life in Cork. The autobiographical element is strong in much working-class fiction; O'Connor wrote on a variety of subjects but his own early life is the basis for dozens of his short stories. His own father, who in times of peace was a labourer, served as a soldier in both the Boer War and the First World War. In one of O'Connor's most famous stories, 'My Oedipus Complex', the central character is born – as O'Connor himself was – when his father is away at war. The father's return precipitates a crisis which is both emotional and financial. The child must now share his mother's attention with his father, now unemployed and not in the best of humour:

> 'Poor Daddy is worried and tired and he doesn't sleep well. . . . You know, don't you, that while he was at the war Mummy got the pennies from the Post Office?'
> 'From Miss MacCarthy?'
> 'That's right. But now, you see, Miss MacCarthy hasn't any more pennies, so Daddy must go out and find us some. You know what would happen if he couldn't? . . . I think we might have to go out and beg for them like the poor old woman on Fridays. We wouldn't like that, would we?'[17]

'My Oedipus Complex' is, like most of O'Connor's stories which depict working-class Cork, humorous rather than grim. The setting is created with great authenticity, and the hardships and limitations of the lives of the poor are not glossed over, but there is nothing in O'Connor's fiction directly comparable to *Children of the Dead End* or 'Hunger', where injustice is the main point of the story. Rather, O'Connor uses the background he knows best as the setting for some personal emotional crisis or development. 'My Oedipus Complex' is a case in point: the danger of having to beg never materializes, and the crisis is resolved – as it was *not* in O'Connor's own life – when a second child is born and father and son, now both pushed out of place, join forces to console each other.

In another story, 'The Man of the House', one finds the same constellation of mother and son; although the father's absence is not accounted for, the boy is of about the age O'Connor would have been when his father was serving in the First World War. In these circumstances, the child must try to take care of his mother when she falls ill – too ill to go to work cleaning Mrs Slattery's house as usual. Sickness often looms large in fictional accounts of working-class life, and the difficulties and prospects for poor people are lightly sketched in: 'To get the doctor I had first to go to

[17]'My Oedipus Complex', in *The Stories of Frank O'Connor* (London, Hamish Hamilton, 1953), p. 9.

the house of an undertaker who was a Poor Law Guardian to get a ticket to show that we couldn't pay. The Poor Law Guardian was very good about that, because afterwards he was sure of the funeral.'[18]

Sent to get cough medicine for his mother, the child meets a little girl who is collecting medicine for her sister who needs 'tonics'; another sister died of consumption a year ago. But no similar disaster awaits the boy; the worst that happens is that the little girl, familiar with the delights of 'cough bottles', entices him into sharing the medicine with her so that there is, at length, none left for his mother; her health is not, however, seriously damaged by the lack. The most lasting effect is that the boy is now wary of 'designing women': 'For years after, when a girl looked at me like that, I hid. I knew by that time what it meant.'[19]

The circumstances of O'Connor's life were in fact much harsher than most of his stories suggest. His father, when not in the army, was given to drinking bouts which could lead to violence. Because of them, financial security was unknown and the only reliable income was that O'Connor's mother earned as a charwoman. She was herself an orphan; degradation was always just a step away and homelessness a spectre. Going to pawn some small household treasure, O'Connor's mother would wrap it in a shawl to conceal it from the neighbours' eyes. This descent from 'hattie' to 'shawlie' marked a distinct downward shift in social status. An acute awareness of such fine gradations is a frequent feature of Irish working-class writing; it points to the ever-present possibility of mobility – in both directions.

Despite the dangers and frustrations of the world of his childhood, O'Connor's writings show it nevertheless to be full of variety, vitality and colour. The visual appeal of Cork is a source of interest and delight; a child can fish in the Glen; bands, made up often of ex-soldiers like O'Connor's father, provide both excitement and a kind of aesthetic education. The countryside, with Irish-speaking districts not far away, is within reach for excursions; the language of the lanes of Cork is full of drama and exuberance.

With the establishment of the Free State, increased opportunities opened for the native Irish; O'Connor, self-educated, was appointed to a librarianship which he himself believed he could never have attained before independence. It provided him with the security and stimulation which made possible his emergence as a writer. But such an advancement up the class ladder points to a paradox. A man who makes a living by writing is not normally regarded as working class, whatever his origins. In Ireland, the class structure is fluid by comparison with that in England, and the picture is further complicated by the persistent features of migration, emigration and unemployment.

A writer like Brendan Behan, while not unique, is something of a rarity in that he was city-born and himself followed the same occupation as his

[18]'The Man of the House', in *Collection Two* (London, Macmillan, 1964), pp. 108–9.
[19]*Op. cit.*, p. 110.

father (house-painting) before he achieved fame as a writer. A much more common pattern is presented by writers like McLaverty and O'Connor. In the usual story, the parents or grandparents moved from the country to the city; the parents (often both mother and father) pursued working-class occupations, frequently a variety of them. The child, who is no doubt clever with books, and words, becomes a clerk or a schoolteacher (like McLaverty) or a minor civil servant. One result is that most of these Irish writers have experienced working-class life domestically, as children, but have no direct experience themselves of working at any manual occupation. There are thus many vivid portrayals of working-class domestic life, but a description of life in the factory or on the construction site is not a particularly common component of Irish working class fiction. Exceptions tend to occur mainly among the Ulster writers, such as Joseph Tomelty (*The Apprentice*) and Ian Cochrane (*A Streak of Madness*).

Patrick MacGill was one who moved upward into journalism; he married well and eventually emigrated to America. In *Children of the Dead End*, he makes a provocative comment about the very poor. The state of being a navvy, he says, is not something which is handed down from father to son, because navvies do not marry and have children. The world Dermod Flynn inhabits in his navvying days is a curiously celibate one, the construction camp a secular and profane parallel to a monastery, depending for its recruits on other people's children. From that dead end, only a very few escape to tell the tale.

Note

Realism comes up all over the place, as an issue, a problem, an aspiration or aversion. It would be virtually impossible to write at any length about fiction without feeling compelled to say something about it. In the background of my own argument, even if at an oblique angle to it, stand such indispensable texts as Ian Watt's *The Rise of the Novel* (London, Chatto and Windus, 1957) and Wayne C. Booth's *The Rhetoric of Fiction* (Chicago, Univ. of Chicago Press, 1961). Of the texts that I refer to explicitly, the Engels letters are in a number of collections, including the useful and wide-ranging *Marx and Engels on Literature and Art* (Moscow, Progress Publishers, 1973). Lukács's *The Historical Novel* is published by Merlin (London, 1962); his *Studies in European Realism* by Penguin (London, 1972). A number of the essays in *Writer and Critic* (London, Merlin, 1978) are relevant too, particularly 'Narrate or Describe' and 'Marx and Engels on Aesthetics'. Influential critiques of 'classic realism', from within a perspective both structuralist and Brechtian, will be found in *Screen* 15:2 (1974) and in *Cinema/Ideology/Politics* (Screen Reader 1, 1977); and there is a very useful summary and development of the arguments in Catherine Belsey's *Critical Practice* (London, Methuen, 1980). Brecht's notes on realism, unpublished in his lifetime, will be found, along with much else of absorbing interest, in *Aesthetics and Politics* (London, Verso, 1980). And I have been heavily indebted throughout to George J. Becker's *Documents of Modern Literary Realism* (Princeton, Princeton U.P., 1963).

9

Unfinished Business: Realism and Working-Class Writing

Tony Davies

> Realism is dependent on the possibility of access to the forces of change in a given moment of history.[1]
>
> The problem of the typical is always a political problem.[2]

'Realism and working-class writing' – every single word presents problems. *Realism* has been one of the major and persistent theoretical contentions of nineteenth- and twentieth-century aesthetics. The political soul, the historical character, the very existence of the *working class* have been, since the thirties, matters of dispute among historians, social scientists and political activists. *Writing*, whether taken in its conceptually sophisticated (French) or descriptively ingenuous (English) sense, remains problematic: alternatively practice, process and product, or all three; avoiding the publicized embarrassments of 'literature' and 'fiction' only at the cost of denominating any distinctive territory of its own.

All these questions have been, and will be, more authoritatively dealt with elsewhere; and though it will hardly be possible to avoid them in this essay, I shall be primarily concerned with the other word in my title – arguably the most difficult one of all, the one around which theoretical issues, social determinations and cultural questions congregate with the greatest practical urgency: the *and* – the relationship, that is, between literary realism and working-class writing.

That relationship, in one strong tradition, is simply taken for granted. According to this view, working-class writing is realistic in the most unpremeditated and unselfconscious fashion: autobiographical, documentary or commemorative, rooted in the experience of family, community, locality, it 'tells it as it is' (or, more often, was) in plain words, valued for their sincerity and simple truth. Taken in itself, this may seem, indeed may actually be, one important historical mode of working-class writing, and a legitimate response to it. In practice, however, it has often taken the form

---

[1] Fredric Jameson, *Marxism and Form* (Princeton, Princeton U.P., 1971), p. 204.
[2] Gyorgy Malenkov, quoted in George J. Becker ed., *Documents of Modern Literary Realism* (Princeton, Princeton U.P., 1963), p. 488.

of a sentimental populism which seeks to conscript a radically simplified and unhistorical conception of the working class, with its sufferings, its struggles, its solidarities, its instinctual loyalties and sturdy common sense, to wider arguments of a markedly reactionary drift: against modernism, for example, or, by a related impulse, against mass-produced, 'commercial' popular culture. For that reason, it is worth noting that this apparently uncomplicated and well-intentioned conception of simple realism is an aesthetic *ideology* with a specific history and discourse, from the Preface to *Lyrical Ballads* to Hoggart's *Uses Of Literacy*: what William Empson has called a contemporary 'version of pastoral'.[3]

Not, of course, an *aesthetic* ideology only. For this view of working-class writing implies a conception of the working class itself, aggregated in traditional industrial communities and extended families, with their associated cultures and repertoires of experience, which, while certainly not entirely false, tends to be static, unhistorical and almost always backward-looking; a conception that quite ignores both the highly varied social, ethnic and occupational composition of the working class and the active and continuously productive nature of experience and its appropriate forms of representation, in constantly changing circumstances: the *making* of the class, in E.P. Thompson's invaluable sense. Thus the static, homogeneous (and, almost always, white and predominantly male) working class of simple proletarian realism is also, recognizably, the subject of certain political ideologies and interpellations: the 'ordinary British voter', this 'great movement of ours', 'the mass of ordinary working people'.

The proximity, here as elsewhere, of aesthetic and political considerations may serve as a reminder that 'realism' is not only a literary-critical term. In a recent discussion of three working-class novelists who started writing 'in a period when experimentation in cultural forms often went hand in hand with revolutionary ideas in politics', Ken Worpole observes that 'that connection has since the Cold War been completely broken', and that 'revolutionary politics has come to be associated with the most dull and unimaginative expectations of what is possible in literature, usually pedestrian verse and prose only distinguished from its 'bourgeois' counterparts by the worthiness of its morality'.[4] This is uncomfortably true; and the related shift in the dominant images and expectations of the political culture can be symbolized by the bovine, incurious 'proles' of Orwell's *Nineteen Eighty Four*: a shift away from the very possibility of revolutionary organization and self-mobilization, and towards the greater pragmatic 'realism' of post-war accommodation and containment, accompanied by a cosy assurance that transformative ideas and prospects may be all very well 'in theory' but that they are 'unrealistic' in practice, and that 'ordinary people' don't want them anyway.

This view of the working class and its wishes, so depressingly characteristic of British labourism, has in its turn, with partial plausibility,

[3]William Empson, *Some Versions of Pastoral* (original edn 1935; London, Penguin, 1966).
[4]Ken Worpole, *Dockers and Detectives* (London, Verso, 1983), p. 92.

been able to invoke a more authentic tradition of proletarian realism: a profound suspicion of bourgeois political ideologies and processes, particularly those that aspire to 'represent' the working class and its interests. Hence that familiar figure in popular folk-lore, the 'typical politician', ambitious, unscrupulous and dishonest, an object of deserved ridicule and contempt, whose generic features (acknowledged in the useful all-purpose imprecation 'typical!') are attested by long traditions of common sense and practical experience.

This may look like the merest irresponsible wordplay, this running-together of the separated senses of familiar words: realism, representation, typicality. But my argument is that it is not, that the string of puns that has constituted itself along this shifting and contested boundary of aesthetics and politics is highly significant, directing attention to questions that remain unanswerable or obscure while the senses are taken separately. The point is not to reduce each and then all of them to a single meaning; still less to translate one set of terms mechanically into the other. But there is nothing at all to be gained from observing the academic protocol that questions of literary genre and tradition are one thing, those of political history and understanding another, and that they should have as little to do with one another as possible. The problem is rather to grasp both the *difference* and the inseparable though shifting kinds of *relatedness* between the terms; not in order to construct another 'theory of realism', but in an attempt to understand how and why a set of meanings mobilized by certain key words has become, historically, the locus of important and still unfinished transactions in the fields of culture and politics: in political culture, in cultural politics.

Realism, representation, typicality: the three words, taken together, recall one of the classical statements:

Realism, to my mind, implies, besides truth of detail, the truthful reproduction of typical characters under typical circumstances. . . . In *City Girl* the working class appears as a passive mass, incapable of helping itself or even trying to help itself. All attempts to raise it out of its wretched poverty come from the outside, from above. This may have been a valid description around 1800 or 1810 in the days of Saint Simon and Robert Owen, but it cannot be regarded as such in 1887 by a man who for almost fifty years has had the honour to participate in most of the struggles of the fighting proletariat and has been guided all the time by the principle that the emancipation of the working class ought to be the cause of the working class itself. The revolutionary response of members of the working class to the oppression that surrounds them, their convulsive attempts – semiconscious or conscious – to attain their rights as human beings, belong to history and may therefore lay claim to a place in the domain of realism.[5]

[5]Friedrich Engels, letter to Margaret Harkness, April 1888, in Becker, pp. 483–5.

This is very familiar; and on one reading it adds up to little more than a naïve argument about *content*: certain things have happened, and should therefore find a place in any novel that aspires to 'truthful reproduction'. It might even be thought rather longwinded, in a self-indulgent way characteristic of the elderly 'General' – the pedantic reference to utopian socialism, the lapse into complacent reminiscence. And it will be readily seen that it makes a 'political' point rather than a 'literary' one, and so perhaps needn't be taken too seriously at all.

But the implied contrast, already noted, between utopian and 'scientific' moments of socialism may suggest that Engels is making (or at least feeling for) an argument of a subtler and more fundamental kind about realism as an historical mode, an argument within which the history, far from being some merely contingent matter of 'authenticity', is quite central: that, insofar as realism is, for the nineteenth century, the preeminent mode of literary representation, it expresses not a moral desideratum or political preference but an indispensable formal condition of its existence as a mode to say that it must stand in some acknowledged and organic relation to the struggles (struggles for *representation*, political, juridical, educational) of the exploited classes. It follows from this that, in spite of enormous pressures to dislodge them or deny their significance (pressures whose strength and urgency can be sensed from the orchestrated public outrage of the Vizetelly affair in the same year as Engels's letter),[6] the truly typical protagonists of late-nineteenth-century realism are the class-conscious worker and the woman struggling to liberate herself from patriarchal oppression – not typical in the sense of most frequent, but because they condense in what Fredric Jameson has called an 'allegorical' figure powerful and necessarily incomplete processes of historical articulation and representation, the coming-to-consciousness of social forces of a fundamental kind.[7]

That, I take it, is the point also, later in the same letter, of the remarks about Balzac, whom Engels calls 'a far greater master of realism than all the Zolas, *passés*, *présents* or *à venir*' – a swipe, perhaps, at Vizetelly, who had sent him a complimentary copy of Margaret Harkness's novel – on the grounds that, 'in spite of his own class sympathies and political prejudices . . . he *saw* the real men of the future where, for the time being, they alone were to be found'.

This is a very powerful argument, which, in spite of its familiarity and its wide influence in Marxist aesthetics, has suggestive implications which have not yet been fully explored. This may be due in part to the casual epistolary tone, and in part to the *form* of some of the statements, with their seemingly-conventional acknowledgement of Balzac's individual 'mastery', his superiority to other writers. Engels's own literary tastes were, as has often been noted, those of a 'cultivated' Victorian gentleman, and some such discrimination is clearly intended. But the mastery is also a

---

[6]See op. cit., pp. 350–82.
[7]Fredric Jameson, *The Political Unconscious* (London, Methuen, 1981), pp. 162ff.

matter of *compulsion*, something not chosen or freely exercised but enforced, against the grain of personal predilection, by circumstances beyond the writer's voluntary control. Thus, alongside a familiar kind of argument about personal 'genius', the Harkness letter suggests another more 'materialist' one, about the objectivity not only of historical processes and situations but also of cultural forms; for what 'compelled' Balzac to deny his own political desires, it is implied, was realism itself.

The relation between realism, as a literary form, and the reality it represents appears, here, rather like that of Marxism, which is after all the healthy child of philosophical realism, and which aims, too, to strip away the superficial appearances of things in order to reveal the real relations of 'typical characters under typical circumstances'. This may remind us that both Marx and Engels spoke highly on several occasions of realist fiction as a mode of social analysis and critique, comparing it favourably to works of sociology and political exegesis. But it recalls too the strong strain of utopianism that, as Jameson has noted, lies at the heart of even the most 'critical' nineteenth-century realism,[8] since the 'typical' may be – perhaps always will be – a prefigurative as well as an allegorical figure. And it secretes a promise. For if in the early years of the century, as Engels suggests, the still 'unmade' working class had no choice but to be represented ('typified') by aristocratic or bourgeois socialists like Owen and Saint Simon; if, 20 years later, it still needed the intermediary spokesmanship of those petty bourgeois revolutionaries of the Cloître Saint-Méry whom Engels calls the 'true representatives of the popular masses'; by the 1880s working people had moved much closer to the point at which 'the emancipation of the working class' would become 'the cause of the working class itself', and would thus soon 'attain their rights as human beings', and 'lay claim to a place' – and no merely subordinate one either – in the domain not of realism only but of reality.

This is a high point of revolutionary optimism, and even the most favourable reading of it is likely, nowadays, to be tinged with irony. Indeed, even in its own terms, as an affirmation of the 'positive moment' of realism, it needs to be read alongside and against Engels's account of the 'negative' one (the terms are Walter Benjamin's[9]) in an earlier letter to Minna Kautsky:

> By consciously describing the real mutual relations, breaking down conventional illusions about them, it shatters the optimism of the bourgeois world, instills doubt as to the eternal character of the existing order.[10]

Needless to say, the two 'moments' of realism, the modes of critique and of

---

[8]*Op. cit.*, pp. 154ff.
[9]Walter Benjamin, letter to Theodor Adorno, in *Aesthetics and Politics* (London, Verso, 1980), p. 140.
[10]Marx and Engels, *On Literature and Art* (Moscow, Progress Publishers, 1973), p. 87.

affirmation, the unmasking of illusion and the celebratory acknowledgement or anticipation of the 'revolutionary response', have for Engels a decisively political, indeed a *class* character. The illusion laid bare is the imagined invulnerability of the *bourgeois* world. And this is not, as has already been noted, simply a contingent matter, the encounter of an existing form (critical realism) with a particular content (bourgeois society). Realism is, inalienably, a form of capitalist society – one of those 'ideological forms' in which, in Marx's famous phrase, people 'become conscious of the conflict and fight it out'.[11] Jameson has written in this context of 'the influence of a given social raw material, not only on the content, but on the very form of the works themselves'.[12] But in truth something even more fundamental is suggested, in Engels's formulations, than 'influence'. The double movement of realism, its generic equivocation between positive and negative moments, false and true totalities, defines it, not as a 'bourgeois genre' in some limiting possessive sense, but as a formal articulation, through the specific and mediated procedures of historical narrative ('typical characters in typical circumstances'), of the lived class relations of capitalist societies.

In one sense such a formulation says very little. Certainly it is useless as a normative or prescriptive definition, which is what some people will always want 'realism' to be. And casually formulated as it is in the two letters it has proved accessible to some decidedly one-sided and tendentious readings. Lukács, for example. The Harkness letter hesitates scrupulously (it is no longer possible unselfconsciously to call this kind of thing 'dialectical') between active and passive modes, a careful registration of differing kinds and levels of determination:

> That Balzac was thus compelled to go against his own class sympathies and political prejudices, that he *saw* the necessity of the downfall of his favourite nobles and described them as people deserving no better fate; that he *saw* the real men of the future where, for the time being, they alone were to be found – that I consider one of the greatest triumphs of realism, and one of the greatest features in old Balzac.

This allows full weight to the individual subjectivity, the writer's singular practice, at the same time as it situates it at the intersection of prepotent historical compulsions and generic determinations. In contrast, though Lukács made the phrase 'triumph of realism' a part of his own vocabulary of approval, his actual elaboration of it, as of other key concepts in the Engels letters, reveals a very different emphasis and purpose.

> What Engels expresses is a simple and clear fact. . . . the uncompromising honesty, free of all vanity, of truly great writers and

---

[11]Marx, *Introduction to the Critique of Political Economy*, in Marx and Engels, *Selected Works* (London, Lawrence and Wishart, 1968), p. 182.
[12]Jameson, *Marxism and Form*, p. 165.

artists. . . . Balzac is defending human integrity in the great capitalist upsurge which began in France during the restoration. . . . With his commitment to man's integrity, he is able to discern the contradictions in the capitalist economic order. . . . There is a victory of realism only when great realist writers establish a profound and serious, if not fully conscious, association with a progressive current in the evolution of mankind.[13]

If Lukács's earlier *Linkskurve* articles betray, in their condemnation of documentary and expressionist forms, too narrowly 'leftist' a conception of proletarian realism, this reading of the Harkness letter graphically demonstrates the consequences of conscripting a theory of realism to a kind of cultural version of the Popular Front – particularly one infiltrated by the disingenuous humanism of the 'cult of personality'. Lukács was writing, in the thirties, under scarcely conceivable pressures and constraints, and easy condemnations are worse than useless. Indeed, even the quoted passage can be read as a coded or 'Aesopian' critique of the Stalinist regime. But the terms of the critique ('uncompromising honesty', 'commitment to man's integrity') betray a fatal capitulation. And only an apologetic parenthesis ('if not fully conscious') betrays Lukács's uneasy recognition of the absurdity of enlisting the old reactionary Balzac to the 'progressive current' of Fourierism, an implausible enterprise, grounded in some imagined 'anti-capitalism' on both sides, that flows directly from the absence of any sense – so strong in Engels – of the determinacy of writing as a practice and of realism as a form. Thus the latter becomes entirely a matter of individual 'honesty', the former nothing more than the 'profound and serious' activity of 'truly great writers and artists', unmediated by language, genre or social situation.

The peculiar and evident limitations of Lukács's writings on realism have been explained in terms of his lifelong devotion to the great nineteenth-century realists (Balzac, Tolstoy), and beyond them to the conceptual categories of German aesthetics (Goethe, Lessing, Hegel). These predilections however, inoffensive enough in themselves, found a powerful reinforcement in Soviet cultural policy, and in particular on the decisive and influential formulations of the first All-Union Congress of Soviet writers in Moscow in the summer of 1934.[14]

It would be quite wrong, as has already been suggested, to identify Lukács unproblematically with the official recommendations of 'socialist realism' – a category that has as little to do with realism as it has with socialism. He continued to argue against them, in an oblique fashion. And in the light of Gorky's assertion, in the central address to the Congress, that critical realism 'did not and cannot serve to educate socialist individuality,

[13]Georg Lukács, 'Marx and Engels on Aesthetics', in *Writer and Critic* (London, Merlin, 1978), pp. 84–5
[14]For a translation of the principal speeches at the Congress, see G. H. Scott, ed., *Problems of Soviet Literature* (Moscow, 1935).

for in criticising everything, it asserted nothing', Lukács's continued championship of the major exemplars of bourgeois realism looks principled, perhaps courageous. None the less, there are substantial grounds of similarity, of a kind that has helped to give currency and authority to a sterile and preemptive attitude to socialist and working-class writing: the common denunciation of the 'sickness' and 'obscenity' of literary modernism, and its categorical separation from realism; the abrupt politicization of writing, as a question of content and of conscious practice; the pervasive idealism and historicism; the sometimes servile deference to the 'truly great' – all these have helped to fix, in the common expectation, an idea of working-class realism as something old-fashioned, unadventurous and dull – and probably, if it calls itself 'socialist', dishonest into the bargain.

Actually, it should be admitted that neither Lukács nor the ideologues of socialist realism have much to say about working-class writing. Karl Radek was taken sharply to task at the 1934 Congress by Willi Bredel and other working-class writers (Bredel had already incurred Lukács's displeasure in his *Linkskurve* period[15]) for his brief and dismissive remarks about existing proletarian fiction. But in retrospect the most significant speech at the Congress was given not by Gorky nor by Radek nor by any of the other writers or critics but by A.A. Zhdanov, Secretary of the Central Committee of the CPSU, who defined the task of socialist realism as 'the ideological remoulding and education of the toiling people in the spirit of Socialism'[16] – a formula not suggestive of any very receptive attitude to the principle that 'the emancipation of the working class ought to be the cause of the working class itself', under whatever social and economic dispensation.

'Enemies of production' – Brecht's phrase for Lukács, Kurella and their associates sticks to Zhdanov too.

> Production makes them uncomfortable. You never know where you are with production; production is the unforeseeable. You never know what's going to come out. And they themselves don't want to produce. They want to play the *apparatchik* and exercise control over other people.[17]

And the dramatist offers, in contrast, his own version of realism:

> Realistic means: discovering the causal complexes of society / unmasking the prevailing view of things as the view of those who are in power / writing from the standpoint of the class which offers the

15'Willi Bredel's Romane', *Linkskurve* (November 1931). *Linkskurve* ('Left Turn') was the journal of the German Association of Proletarian Revolutionary Writers. See *Aesthetics and Politics*, p. 60, and Jurgen Rühle, *Literature and Revolution* (London, Pall Mall Press, 1969), pp. 161–4, for brief accounts of this period.
16Scott, p. 21.
17Walter Benjamin, conversation with Brecht, in *Aesthetics and Politics*, p. 97.

broadest solution for the pressing difficulties in which human society is caught up/emphasizing the element of development/making possible the concrete and making possible abstraction from it.[18]

The affinities of this with the Engels letters need no emphasis. But the divergencies are striking too; and his conception of realism not as a form or genre, still less as an archive of achieved and exemplary masterpieces (a 'Valhalla of the enduring figures', as Brecht called it elsewhere[19]), but rather as a productivity of historical narratives and meanings provides an instructive point from which to assess the fate of the concept both in eastern Europe, where Brecht is admired, when he is, as a great proletarian realist, and in the West, where he has in recent years been adopted as the patron of a deconstructive anti-realist modernism.[20] Behind this lies a more general polarization: on the one hand (east and west), an elephantine bureaucratic centralism, on the other, a fevered leftist avant-gardism. Both would call themselves socialist. Both aspire to historical 'typicality' and centrality, recalling Perry Anderson's observation that 'in the twentieth century political parties present themselves as collective agents *par excellence* – endowed with a high degree of volition, intention and clearly articulated goals'.[21] And both claim, in that spirit, to represent the working class – to 'act for it', as we say, in a usage at once theatrical and forensic.

Acting – the Aristotelian *mimesis* – is a central category for theories of literary representation. The characters and narratives of realist fiction are, to use Hardy's word, 'enactments';[22] and it is suitably a playwright who has insisted, in the name of realism, that fictional representation, like acting, is no simple matter of transcription or mechanical mimicry but a complex and mediated process of transformation, a 'production'. It is in this sense that all prescriptive definitions and bureaucratic legislations of 'realism' and its supposed antonyms can properly be described as 'enemies of production' – as inimical to the dynamic and protean forms, to the developing social relations that arise from all productive activity. But production, like acting, is also a form of illusion. Just as the wealth-producing processes of capitalist society, and the forms of labour and exploitation that they mobilize, mysteriously vanish into their products, to reappear magically transformed into commodities, so too the 'products' – narratives, images, meanings – of cultural and creative processes can come to seem absolute, self-created, offering themselves for consumption in the legitimated modes of appreciation, instruction and pleasure.

---

[18]Bertolt Brecht, 'Popularity and Realism', in *Aesthetics and Politics*, p. 82.
[19]*Op. cit.*, p. 77.
[20]See, for example, *Screen* (summer 1974), special issue on 'Brecht and Revolutionary Cinema'.
[21]Perry Anderson, 'Communist Party History', in *People's History and Socialist Theory* (London, Routledge, 1981), pp. 154–5.
[22]'Real enactments of the intensest kind' – Thomas Hardy, *Jude the Obscure*, part II, chapter VI.

It is this process of transformation into cultural commodities, and its accompanying ideologies of aesthetic consumption, that are disrupted by the Brechtian emphasis. The striking thing about the definition of realism quoted earlier is that it is in fact no definition at all, but rather a set of suggestive injunctions whose participial form insists on movement and uncompleted action just as its deliberately paratactic structure (a loose assemblage of modernist slogans; a cinematic montage) refuses to assign syntactical or formal priorities. Indeed, the only element of it that carries any demonstrable formal implications is the third: 'writing from the stand-point of the class which offers the broadest solutions to the pressing difficulties in which human society is caught up'. Here, the central aesthetic concept of 'point of view' is brought face to face with the Marxist notion of class-standpoint, an encounter in which the former is 'politicized' only to the extent of being pressed to declare its already powerful, though generally latent, moral and political inclinations. And even this, insofar as it predicates anything by way of 'typical characters in typical circumstances', is far from narrowly prescriptive, given the wide variety of techniques already available from bourgeois realism (and even more from the modernist repertoire) for the presentation of fictional points of view.[23] What the confrontation does do, however, is to 'lay claim to a place in the domain of realism', not for some new 'proletarian' version of the bourgeois protagonist or the old, confident omniscient narrator, but for a range of 'points of view' that may, within new institutions of distribu-tion, reading, discussion, decisively reformulate through a series of 'alienation-effects' the narratives, the problems, the available and con-ceivable resolutions of a pertinent and answerable realism.

Why 'realism'? Why retain, for what must be a very different, a radically decentred practice, a concept whose historical attributes and formal predispositions seem to gravitate inescapably towards textual and ideological centrings: typical protagonists, dominant points of view, dis-cursive hierarchies,[24] theoretical prescriptions, bureaucratic imperatives? Whose utopian daydreams and obscurest objects of desire, however pleasurably 'subversive', avert their faces from the necessary world of con-tradiction, difficulty, change? Whose plausible impersonations – even in the name of liberty – compel us to adopt the obsequious passivity of a 'reading'? On this point, Brecht's refusal, in spite of his distaste for Lukács and notwithstanding his own close association with expressionist and objectivist forms, to abandon realism, his insistence on its continuing importance as 'a major political, philosophical and practical issue . . . a matter of general human interest' are worth emphasizing, not as a model to be slavishly imitated or an incitement to stale partisanship but as a

---

[23]For this concept, see Wayne C. Booth, *The Rhetoric of Fiction* (Chicago, Univ. of Chicago Press, 1961).
[24]For an account of realism in these terms, see Colin MacCabe, 'Realism and the Cinema: some Brechtian theses', in *Screen* (summer 1974), p. 8.

reminder that realism, in all its multiple incarnations, is not really a literary form or genre on movement or tradition at all but a contested space, the scene of an unfinished argument.

Defined in this way, realism is likely to appear, from a literary-critical point of view, little more than an attitude, a pious hope without substance or consistency. But the business of working-class writing never did look, from that point of view, particularly important or even real. Leavis's sneer about 'the duty of the writer to identify himself with the working class',[25] and his contemptuous assignation of such self-evident *bêtises* to the 'Marxizing' thirties, are typical enough, and point to a general abandonment of the issues, as well as to a dyspeptic and complacent parochialism that is specially English. In the post-war years, when not only working-class writing but the working class itself has been widely reported to be little more than a sentimental anachronism, literary criticism has gone about its business, 'placing' here and 'evaluating' there, very busily and self-importantly indeed. Only recently has it started to develop headaches, and to sleep badly at nights. But it is not thought that this has anything to do with the unfinished business of realism, or with bad dreams about the working class.

In the meantime, in contrastingly modest and inconspicuous ways, with small resources, working on the margins or beyond the edges of official notice and toleration, groups of people have begun over the past decade or so to reinvestigate for themselves the possibility of a working-class writing, and the appropriate forms and occasions; meeting in schoolrooms and libraries, in WEA and extramural classes, in Liverpool, Bristol, Birmingham, London. Often the enterprise has involved conjunctions of memory and desire, youth and age, the unearthing of half-lost continuities and their reconnection to an imagined future. In some instances – women's writing, local history – the work produced has started to engage the attention of a larger public. And more recently many of these groups have linked up, through Community Arts Associations or the Federation of Worker Writers, into wider networks of performance, publication and discussion, within which, in quite different circumstances but with a strong sense of the relevant history, the unfinished business is being taken up again.[26]

In a difficult, obliquely-argued, interesting rumination on proletarian literature as a 'version of Pastoral', William Empson has written of 'the tone of humility normal to pastoral', noting that it is 'very well suited to a socialist society'.[27] He is thinking of the conscious humility of the courtly or bourgeois intellectual 'imagining the feelings of the simple person' – the peasant or worker; and this suggests that his conception of socialist society,

[25]F. R. Leavis, 'Literature and Society' (1943), in *The Common Pursuit* (London, Penguin, 1962), p. 182.
[26]For an account of these developments, see Ken Worpole and Dave Morley, eds., *The Republic of Letters* (London, Comedia, 1982).
[27]Empson, *Pastoral*, pp. 16–17.

and of the intellectual within it, may owe more to Ruskin or Tolstoy than to Marx. But it is true, none the less, that most working-class writing does display a notable modesty, a disinclination to posture and whine, a preference for the humorous and deprecating not always to be observed in writing *about* it – this one included. This has absolutely nothing to do with some imagined habit of deference or *ressentiment* – the predominant bourgeois typifications of working-class mentality. But it hasn't got much to do, either, with the Promethean beefcake of official 'proletarian realism'. It represents in individuals a collective and historical awareness (for the consciousness of an exploited class *is* its history) of difficult but sustaining traditions of survival and resistance.

Those traditions have often seemed to people who (sometimes through that process of social mobility known as 'becoming a writer') have distanced themselves from them, to be dying or dead; and many of the better-known records of them, from that isolated and retrospective standpoint (*Love on the Dole*, say, or, in a different mode, *The Uses of Literacy*), have been elegiac, pessimistic, obituary. But historical classes, and their transmitted forms of knowledge, feeling and identity, do not simply die away, any more than they remain forever embalmed in some ideal (cloth-capped, moleskin-trousered) literary incarnation. But the Women's Movement has offered a reminder, in recent years, that a collective consciousness, if it is to be active and useful, has to be built and defended: recovered from the past, redefined and consolidated in the present. This is not, needless to say, a question of 'literature', and literary critics will not on the whole find it very interesting. But it is very much a question of *writing*, both existing and still to be done; and it calls not for the prescriptive formal realism of the professional critic, nor for the cynical political realism of the bureaucrat, but for the open-minded critical realism of those for whom, in the end, reality holds nothing to be frightened of.

Note

Life

Born in September 1916 in Shildon, county Durham, into a mining family, Sid Chaplin left school at 14 years of age to train as a colliery blacksmith. He completed his apprenticeship with a year at Fircroft Workingmen's College, Birmingham. Returning to the colliery he served underground as a conveyor mechanic and for several years as secretary of his local union lodge. Brought into contact with the wider aspects of the mining industry as chief reporter for the National Coal Board (NCB) magazine *Coal*, he travelled the coalfields of Britain, Eire and the United States, and as trade unionist achieved the unusual double of holding office in the National Union of Journalists (NUJ) as well as the National Union of Mineworkers (NUM).

His first collection of short stories, *The Leaping Lad*, won an Atlantic Award in Literature and this, together with his novel *The Thin Seam*, provided the basis for Alan Plater's much acclaimed musical, written with Alex Glasgow, *Close the Coalhouse Door*. (London, Methuen playscripts, 1969) Translations of his novels have appeared in French, German, Czech and Russian. Awarded an OBE for his services to the arts, in particular his work for Northern Arts, Sid Chaplin is also an Honorary MA of the University of Newcastle, and in 1977 was made an Honorary Fellow of Sunderland Polytechnic.

Novels

My Fate Cries Out (London, Phoenix House, 1949).
The Thin Seam (London, Phoenix House, 1949; Oxford, Pergamon, 1968).
The Big Room (London, Eyre and Spottiswoode, 1960).
The Day of the Sardine (London, Eyre and Spottiswoode, 1961).
The Watchers and the Watched (London, Eyre and Spottiswoode, 1962).
Sam in the Morning (London, Eyre and Spottiswoode, 1965).
The Mines of Alabaster (London, Eyre and Spottiswoode, 1971).

Short Stories

The Leaping Lad (London, Phoenix House, 1946; London, Longman, 1970).
On Christmas Day in the Morning (Ashington/Machester, MidNAG/Carcanet, 1978).
The Bachelor Uncle (Ashington/Manchester, MidNAG/Carcanet, 1980).

Essays

The Smell of Sunday Dinner (Newcastle, Frank Graham, 1971).
A Tree with Rosy Apples (Newcastle, Frank Graham, 1972).
'Durham Mining Villages', in M. Bulmer, ed., *Mining and Social Change* (London, Croom Helm, 1978).

Anthology

Us Northerners, ed. with Arthur Wise, (London, George Harrap, 1970).

10

The Making of a Working-Class Writer: An Interview with Sid Chaplin

Michael Pickering and *Kevin Robins*

Question (Q): Could you begin by telling us how your early life in the Durham pit village contributed to your development as a writer?

Sid Chaplin (SC): Well, it was extraordinarily rich. Everybody lived together, everybody had everything in common. They were real communities, you know, and there was real loyalty in the street. The street came first. But after the street came the village, and the village was supported by the pit, and your pit was the best pit of all. But at the same time it was an environment with all kinds of dichotomies. Newfield is the best example. You had your club men and your chapel men, solid temperance men. The club men only went to chapel for anniversaries and harvest festivals. They might go at Christmas as well. But both the chapel men and the club men were marvellous talkers. I remember they still had the old ranters. They made pit-life stories of all the parables. I can remember one old bearded preacher opening the bible, and without looking at it, saying 'My text for today is from the Gospel of John, chapter one, verse one: In the beginning was the Word, and the Word was with God, and the Word was God'. And then he preached a sermon without a note. I thought how marvellous! But the thing that stuck in my mind was 'In the beginning was the Word' and that there was something holy about the word.

    The sneck-watchers waiting for the pub or club to open, waiting for the click of the sneck indicating that the bolt had been withdrawn, they.'d sit on their hunkers. We'd be playing marbles or tops – or whatever the season indicated, because there was a game for every season – and somebody would start off story-telling. 'Well, I mind . . .' And I would listen to it all. Apart from that I had a couple of uncles who were great story-tellers. It used to be gala day when they came to our house. One of them was my Uncle George, who was a pit electrician like my dad. We didn't see him very often, because he also worked a lot of overtime. He told a very good story. And then there was my Uncle Fred, who was a brass bandsman. He came often. He used to play the village bandstands, every Sunday. He was the only fellow who was allowed to sit on our table. We used to have an oilcloth-covered table in those days, excepting on Sunday when we had a velvet cloth. Even my houseproud mother was so enthralled by him that she ignored the fact that he was sitting on the table.

Q: Can we ask you to expand on the significance of the oral tradition? You have described the pit village environment as 'a good forcing ground for the imagination', because at 'the street corner or in the chapel, in kitchen or in the lodge meeting, you learned the point and pith, the power and sanctity of the word'. How did this influence you as an emergent writer?

SC: Well, because it was material and it stuck. Sometimes you didn't use it. Sometimes it was important because it was about the history of your own people. I remember round about 1924 being taken for walks by a chap who was a winding engineman, and one day we were walking towards a little village over the river called Willington. I said, 'It always looks nice at Willington, till you get there'. He says, 'You're right lad. I'll tell you a story about Willington'. He told me the story of Straker and Loves forcing the miners to rock the tubs after they'd filled them – sway on them is the miner's term – to settle the coal down so there would be more coal for the Master. The miners refused to obey this ruling. They went out on strike, and they were all evicted. The candyman came in and evicted the families. They were in the fields for about 30 weeks, under sheets and blankets, stretched from the hedges. He told me this story, and it wasn't until I was about 16 or 17 that somebody loaned me a copy of Fynes's *The Miners of Northumberland and Durham*. He'd told the story to me as something that had happened to his father, and it was very immediate. Now here was a history book telling me about it, and the Rocking Strike happened, if my memory serves me right, in about 1862 or 1863.

Q: Was it the content of the local oral tradition, or was it the quality of the spoken word which influenced you most?

SC: Partly the content, yes, and partly the way it was told. They were marvellous story-tellers. In fact, first of all I wanted to be a raconteur. I found out that I always missed the point of any story I was telling. Partly the reason that I'm a writer is that you can be more sure of getting the story right in writing it down, whereas a raconteur, you know, it just drops off his lips. It's the greatest art, oral story-telling, no doubt about it. But I haven't got the performer's ability; it's got to be born in you.

Q: Your stories draw upon the folklore tradition of the mining villages, coming from your experience of growing up in what you have described as 'a closed kind of world where folklore was not yet a subject but a second set of references'. Yet there are also literary influences. What

would you say was the balance of influence from folklore and from
literary tradition in your work?

SC: The kind of folklore I was interested in was contemporary folklore, like
the tale of the Leaping Lad, for instance, which must have happened
before World War I. He was a fellow called Jumper Craig really. A man
told it to me down the pit, and he says, 'This'll mak' thee a good story'. I
said, 'Did this fellow actually exist? And did he try to kill the judge?'
'Haway', he says, 'he never got anywhere near him'. But, of course,
that's what makes the writer. You immediately seize on the point. That
was the kind of folklore I was interested in. That was the kind of story
which my own folk had considered valuable enough to pass on down.

My reading – to turn to the question of literary influences – really
began to expand when I walked into the Spennymoor Settlement,
having heard that they had a very good branch library there. Bill and
Betty Farrell not only ran the library but advised on books, and it was
then that I began to read Hemingway, Ralph Fox, H.E. Bates, Ernst
Toller, Huxley, and began to dive deeper into French and Russian
writers like Barbusse, Zola and (towards the end of the war)
Gorky – after first seeing the Russian film trilogy of *My Universities* etc.
Bill Farrell was very friendly with A.E. Coppard, the short-story writer.
He produced plays and eventually built his Everyman's Theatre, which
meant that by my mid twenties I had seen most of Sean O'Casey, a lot of
Strindberg, Priestley, and, as well as Synge, a good many other Irish
plays. So if the pit – and smithy – were *my* universities, the Settlement
was my finishing school. It was Bill Farrell, in fact, who read and praised
my first one-act play, helped me to revise it, and got the Durham Left
Book Club Theatre to take it up. It was entitled *Half-Hour Hell* and,
although it was never in fact produced, it received an honorable mention
from the judges of a Unity Theatre competition.

Q: Could you outline for us the stages by which you got into writing?

SC: The writing really began about the time I became an apprentice blacksmith at the colliery. I was lucky enough to have an old Scotsman, Alex
Wyley, as my smith. I was his striker and his apprentice. We worked
three shifts, five o'clock in the morning, seven o'clock, and three o'clock
in the afternoon. This meant that two weeks out of every three we were
virtually alone. In fact, the anvil and your job was a little oasis. Alex was
a remarkable, self-educated man. He'd started as a country blacksmith
and as a farrier, then found his way to the collieries. He started at Castle
Eden where his father was a gardener. He knew the whole of Burns and
Walter Scott. In addition to that he was a WEA student. The first thing
he achieved with me is that he got me to go to the WEA, two weeks out
of every three. I spent a bit of time before I found the class that appealed
to me. This was in Ferryhill. Eventually I found an extra-mural class, and
the first tutor was a man called A.P. Rossiter, who was a poet and had

worked with Ogden on basic English. He was a very fine tutor indeed, a very stimulating man. A bit Shavian in the way he tackled subjects, and he certainly surprised you out of your stupor – because remember pretty often I'd started work at five o' clock in the morning, had a nap, got up and had my tea, and then gone out. If I'd been working overtime, then there wasn't much nap. It was a job to keep awake. I'm sure he noticed, because I used to sit with my head in my hands, especially when it came to Jane Austen! But on the whole he gave some very stimulating lectures, and the discussions were good afterwards. I became a member of the WEA and went on their tours to local historic places, and went also to the occasional summer school. That gave me a start. The next tutor I had was Dr Leach, who was absolutely the contrary of Rossiter. Rossiter was out to jerk you into thinking, Leach was much milder, much more conventional.

The next thing that happened was that I heard about the Spennymoor Settlement. Here I was among people who were great readers, and great lovers of books, and who liked a good argument about them. All this was going on, and what I often used to do, when I was on the afternoon shift, was to go down this little country lane to Strawberry Cot. I remember there were just the ruins of the cottage – people had been taking stones away. There was an elderberry tree and an old lilac tree. This was a great period for me for being loaned books, and for picking up books in second-hand shops, and I can remember reading Browning there for the first time (including *The Ring and the Book*), and Walt Whitman, who was *my* poet. I recognized a person like myself in Walt Whitman, a kindred spirit. He was a working man. I knew that from the start, it came out of everything in his poetry. A working man with a great feeling for his fellow working men, and fellow citizens as well when it came to the Civil War. I can distinctly remember that it almost seemed arranged as the proper stage-setting: the lilac was in bloom, and I first read 'When Lilacs Last in the Dooryard Bloomed' in the garden of that ruined cottage. After that I wanted to be a poet!

Q: Did you write poetry?

SC: Yes, I wrote poetry, but after a time I realized that poetry requires absolute dedication, and it's the kind of dedication that should start early – dedication to the word and to the muse. I was writing mainly free verse, and simple metrical verse. I realized after a while that I hadn't time enough to devote myself to it. Also I'd started too late.

Q: Was it your reading of all the books that you were now being introduced to which first stimulated you into trying your hand at writing?

SC: It was a combination of the story-telling that went on around me all the time, and reading. If I owe anything to A.P. Rossiter, and to a certain degree also to Leach, it is that they were both insistent on getting it right,

right in both word and spirit, what I was putting down, coming out of all this material around me in the story-telling tradition.

Q: How did you come to make the transition from poetry to writing fiction?

SC: I began by writing essays on poets for local newspapers and small journals. There was a little tuppenny magazine called the *North Eastern Weekly Gazette*. I did an essay for them on John Greenleaf Whittier, but I never got round to doing one on Whitman, because Whitman seemed too sacred a subject to touch, and I was so inadequate. But they were good to me, and I was earning right from the start, half a crown a time, a postal order for a paper written by the people for the people. It had a cheap red cover, you could see the first white page through the red cover, it was so thin and cheap. It was very exciting. The foreshift was my favourite writing time. I used to come in and get a bath in front of the fire, in time-honoured fashion, get my meal, then go to bed and write with a pen and pad. Of course a few things went into limbo and I never heard of them again. I think the first thing was a short story, I can't even remember the title now, but it was a pit-life adaptation of a Jerome K. Jerome play. I never thought in terms of becoming a professional writer. In the first place it was somehow feminine, that's why it had to be a secret occupation with me. It wasn't until I got my first postal order for half a crown that my mother found out, and then the whole family. I wrote completely under pseudonyms the whole three years until I came out of my apprenticeship, so nobody ever knew excepting the immediate family. That was the feeling you got in a mining village, a man found his place through his muscular strength and ability, or agility. Same whether it was the big hewer, or a good footballer, or a breeder of pigeons, or a leekman. These were masculine things, and writing was very effeminate, so I said nothing about it. So the idea of becoming a professional writer then would just have been a wild dream. That was my start at writing, though of course you could say my real start was at school, with a teacher astute enough to look at a rather dull, freckle-faced boy and see that there was something in him. I'm sure that if it hadn't been for this teacher, Rupert Wilkinson, I wouldn't have had the same impetus, because it was such a terrible jump, even to do this secret writing. I think I went to the pillar box about six times before I parted with my first piece, and then I felt rather relieved when I never heard about it again.

Q: How did you finally come to make your break with the mining community?

SC: Well, what happened was that I went away to college. This was in the late 1930s, still a period of high unemployment, and because of that economics, and subjects related to it, were very popular, as you can well understand. So when I put in for a sholarship I put in for one at Fircroft College in Birmingham to do economics and political theory. What a stewing I had! Having left school at 14, and having attended so many schools, I didn't have much of a grounding. I just hadn't been trained in thinking. You can say what you like about the advantages or disadvantages of various forms of education, but I think the point about public school and university education is that at their best they teach you to think. It's only very rarely that you are taught to think in a working-class school, and I think it's still true today. Anyway, that was my greatest deficiency. I remember an old collier manager at my grandad's pit. If the scores were coming out well he used to come home singing 'Lily of Laguna' and slashing down all the thistles and nettles and dandelions – and he never missed, he sliced through them like magic! It's that kind of debonair physical action that I've always wanted to emulate in the realm of thinking. But with me the action has got to be brick by brick; I'm a bit thick really, a bit thick and rather dislocated in my thoughts.

Q: So you found studying at college quite a struggle?

SC: Yes, certainly a struggle, but they were very kind to me. The economics tutor was a man called Warburton who had been a Fircroft student himself; he'd written a history of the potters' union. He was a marvellous man, a marvellous teacher. I had to do an essay at the end of my first term, and he dodged me for about three weeks, I couldn't get hold of him to get to know his verdict on this essay. I finally nobbled him in his study. He used to smoke this big Sherlock Holmes pipe. It was supposed to hold an ounce of tobacco, that was the legend. He filled it in the morning, he lit it at his bedside and it sat, still going, beside his porridge at breakfast time, and it never went out till he went to bed again. I nobbled him in his study and I said, 'What about that economics essay of mine?' He blew out a cloud of smoke and I could see his eyes twinkling. He said, 'Sid, there's one thing I can say for you, your economics may be inexact, but they're jolly entertaining! And anybody who can make economics entertaining is wasting his time.' So I didn't offically switch to English Literature, but they made things easy for me, and I more or less spent most of my time in the library.

Here I did some writing. I wrote a story there and sent it to a magazine called *Breakaway*, which was a quarterly. It was accepted, and on the strength of its acceptance I got a year's subscription, 7s 6d, a lot of money. I think it was due to come out in the third issue, and it went bust after the second! But it was an encouragement you see. That was the first serious story I wrote. I went on to write a lot of short stories during the war. Everyone was writing short stories then; it was a time for a great flowering of the short story. Nobody had much time I suppose. Everybody was being chased from their jobs into the army or into other places of work, and these little magazines sprang up like mushrooms. Dozens and dozens. Three I remember in particular: *Penguin New Writing, Modern Reading* and *Seven*. They were literally my training school. It was a great time for periodicals, small periodicals existing on very small circulations. *Seven* was exceptional. They got up to about 100,000 at their peak, and the stories were never much more than a thousand words each. That was their formula. And they were all from ordinary folk. They're still worth reading, and I still see some of my old fellow contributors coming up in all sorts of posh places now.

Q: When you were first starting to write, having come from a working-class background, were you aware of other working-class writers?

SC: Yes, very early on. Another way of getting a further education was at Adult Schools – secular versions of the Friends' Meeting Houses – and you went along and got a handbook, there was a lesson every week. They had an expert in to give it, and then there would be a rattling good discussion. I was a member of two, one at Windlestone and one at Shildon, where my uncle was a leading member. This one at Shildon was particularly good. I'd be no more than about 17 when I went. I remember, after one meeting, saying to a fellow called Enoch Goynes, who was an engine driver: 'Boy, have you read *The Everlasting Mercy*? Absolutely marvellous'. Masefield, you know. 'Tha come down to our house', he said, 'and ah'll give tha a book that knocks Masefield into a cocked hat'. He took me to his house, and he gave me a paper-covered first edition of *The Widowing of Mrs Oldroyd*. I used to stay with my uncle all day, I had my bike and I can remember setting off about six o'clock and stopping at a street called Cobbler's Hall, and dying to look at this book, you know. I just sat down and read it there, on the dyke side. I'd never come across anything like this before. I knew about Jack Lawson, and I'd read *A Man's Life*. I also knew about Cronin, and had read *The Stars Looked Down* in the *Daily Herald*. But all that paled into insignificance as I sat there reading. It was a major event in my life.

Q: Did you see yourself from the start as a working-class writer?

SC: Yes, yes, but at the same time with enough dignity and presumption, you might say, to see myself as a writer without any label.

Q: Did you try to break into any literary circles?

SC: Well, I was completely different to Jack, Jack Common, in that respect. The only circle I was a member of was John Lehmann's. He was very affable, and every now and again when I went to London I went to see him or to a committee meeting of a little organization called Eighteen Plus, one of those hopeful wartime organizations for a better world to come. I was on the executive committee. But Lehmann was always good to me, always generous, sending books and writing notes – he never rejected anything out of hand. The extraordinary thing is that the first acceptance from John Lehmann was for three poems. Almost within weeks of sending them off, I wrote a sketch called 'Coal is the Story' – it's in *The Smell of Sunday Dinner* – and I sent it to *Horizon*. I got a very nice letter back from Cyril Connolly, saying sorry, not exactly my cup of tea, I hope you won't mind my having sent it to John Lehmann. That was great, because John Lehmann had just accepted the poems. When he was presented with a piece of prose he jumped at it.

Q: Could you tell us of your experiences during the war, and how you became established as a journalist and as a writer?

SC: It's difficult for any isolated writer – and any working-class writer is by definition isolated. I would think they are even more isolated today, when the equivalents of the little magazine are radio, which is relatively easy, and television, which is terribly difficult to get in. It was at that time an extraordinary period, a flowering of little magazines, covering the whole political spectrum. Bishop Auckland was our nearby town, and every time I went into Bishop Auckland there seemed to be a new magazine in the bookshop there, on the stall. It was really wonderful. There was a period when they had a little reviews anthology, which came out annually, and that went on for seven or eight years, towards the end of the war and just after. It was as if the war was a great leveller. We were all folk in danger of death; class distinction seemed to disappear, and everybody had to have a voice. Mind, this effort to give people a voice was of course greatly assisted by a generation of left-wing public school-boys, like John Lehmann, Cyril Connolly, Reginald Moore, and so on. It was very exciting. You knew your markers, those you had to write up to; you were competing with the best people. You might very well be published alongside Auden or Spender or V. S. Pritchett. There was *Tribune* as well of course, with a great literary editor in George Orwell. When he eventually left, the magazine continued to be inclined in Orwell's direction. It was as if he had set it on a course that it couldn't deviate from. The sky was the limit then. I remember reading Orwell in *Tribune*, in the early days of the war, he used to do a regular column, 'As I Please'. I used to regard him then as a great master of English prose. Cobbett's *English Grammar* was, I suppose, originally my great yard-stick. One of the things that happened to me early on was picking up, for about tuppence, a copy of it. I got my English from that Grammar. Orwell seemed to me to fulfil the requirement demanded of good prose. I was terribly excited when he asked me to fill in as *Tribune*'s columnist for a couple of weeks while he was on holiday. I was going down to a meeting one weekend, and daft fool that I was, I didn't drop him a line, though I had every intention of going to see him. He lived in a little mews somewhere. I found it alright, and it appeared very posh to me, with geraniums on the window sill and a brightly polished doorknob and letterbox. But I couldn't get an answer. So I never met George Orwell! He took essays on poetry. I once wrote an article about Synge and Wilfred Owen, taking the introductions to the volumes of their poems as my basis. He gave it a complete backpage. That was terribly exciting for a young writer. There's nothing like it today. It's the only time we've ever had anything like a free voice in writing, the only time I know when it's been like that for working-class writers. It was a kind of socialism in writing.

Q: So it was a very democratic period in terms of the politics of writing?

SC: Certainly, certainly. I know it had happened in some ways before, but it was all so exuberant, and the very fact that there was a shortage of paper made it all the more exciting. But as for becoming a member of any literary circle, everything seemed to go wrong for me, like with the visit to Orwell's house. It was because I didn't understand the background of these people; you couldn't just call round as with my pit folk and expect them to be in. Orwell was probably away for the weekend. But it was also diffidence, and a feeling of inadequacy. When I got into the company of people like Roy Campbell, Geoffrey Grigson and Dylan Thomas, instead of talking, I listened. When it came to bashing something out on your typewriter and getting it published, there was no great gap between the two. There's never been a time when, given the talent, any writer anywhere could get into print better than the war period and just after. When television came that was the end of it.

Q: Could we just go back a bit? What happened after you finished working as a blacksmith, what did you go on to do then?

SC: I remember a fellow called Teddy Shields, the third time I went back to the pit after leaving, saying, 'Tha's like a bloody yo-yo, lad'. What happened was that the Rockefeller Foundation, round about 1946, had started giving prizes, so many a year. I think they were all much the same. Mine was £300. You could call them either Rockefeller prizes or Atlantic awards. £300 was a year's wages at that time. I sat down with that to write my first novel, *My Fate Cries Out*. At the behest of my publisher at the time, John Baker, I wrote a novel about nationalization. It was a mess and I knew it, but I sent it off. He returned it double-quick and said it was no good. I said to hell with you, I'm going to write to enjoy myself. I sat down then and wrote *My Fate Cries Out*. A lot of people still remember that novel with affection, even though it's so long ago. It's the only one that's never been reprinted.

When I came back from the college (I know this is a very confused story I'm telling you), when I came back, I hoped I'd get a job as a blacksmith again. The engineer said, 'There isn't a fire available, lad. But there are some jobs underground as belt-fitters'. I got a job underground doing that, and that was a god-send as far as writing was concerned. I'd been down the pit on a weekend basis before, and had the odd trip in at other times, but this was seven days a week, going on during the war. As fitters we weren't confined to one spot. We went to all the places there were conveyors. I really got to know mining inside out, including the new form of mechanized mining that was coming in at that period. In the early days they elected me secretary of the local Mechanics Lodge. I had about three years of that. That was a great experience because, along with the men's problems, you got a lot of anecdotes and such. But the best experience of all was simply working down the pit. Men would put their lamps face down in the dust and say, 'I mind once . . .' and you'd get a story. It was absolutely great. Taking my material from miners like that at first hand strengthened my resolve to be true to the spirit as well as the letter of what I was writing.

After that dud novel about nationalization came back I had about three months left out of the year covered by the money from the prize. I started *My Fate Cries Out* then. It was a marvellous feeling; it was like touching bottom in a swimming pool and then feeling yourself going up. I knew after failure that I was in the process of writing a real novel, a real story. Unlike the other one, it just seemed to flow out of me, and it had depth, again unlike the other one which was just surface writing – it had been about things I knew but hadn't been interested enough in them to plumb.

After that I wrote *The Thin Seam*, then I was offered a job as a reporter on *Coal* magazine. I was there about five years, and I should think I went down about 300 pits, because I always insisted on going down the pits. I never got rid of that romantic feeling I had as a kid; every pit I went to was different, and every pit had a fascination for me. I covered three major disasters. Perhaps that was a bad thing from my point of view, because after experience of them I've never wanted to write a novel about a pit disaster – I'd been too close to what it was really like.

Apart from journalism I did no writing at all for about nine years. Then I got a job as public relations officer up here in Newcastle for the Coal Board. That kept me very busy, but at least I wasn't travelling then. I had home as a fixed and steady point. That meant I was able to write again, and it was then that the second stage of my writing career began. It was while living in Newcastle that I wrote two novels that were set in the city, in Elswick and Byker. The first of these novels was about a city being pulled down, with the old streets and the old communities disappearing, and what this meant for working-class kids, their problem of rootlessness. The second one was about a young man on the west side of Elswick, in a working-class community, starting his married life and sloughing off his old pals one by one. I think that what I tried very hard to capture, in the Newcastle novels, is the strength of family life and street life, here in the town, and I tried to show how that was disappearing, going to waste. I tried to convey this fragmentation of working-class communities after the war, the experience of young lads leaving school at 16 and unemployed – and it was a period when my own kids were teenagers. I wanted to record it. At the same time, just as employment seemed to be growing scarce, we knew for a certainty that the major industries – not only coal but steel and shipbuilding – were sliding away. And the street system, which was the community system of the city and the surroundings of the city, that was going away as well. And I just wanted to record it, an awful lot of that was drawn from life.

Q: When you were writing those two Newcastle novels – *The Day of the Sardine* and *The Watchers and the Watched* – were you conscious of any affinity with other writers who were writing during the same period about working-class experience of social change – Sillitoe, Braine or Barstow, for example?

SC: *The Day of the Sardine* wasn't out when I first met Stan Barstow, John Braine, Keith Waterhouse and Len Doherty. This was the early days of television, around 1962, and we all met together. It was a riotous evening. Keith Waterhouse is a marvellously funny writer, but he's not funny in real life, John Braine is the funny one. We all got together, and we made this television programme. We became the Northern writers mafia for a time. My particular friend was Stan Barstow.

Q: A more general question . . . what do you see as the social and political role of the writer?

SC: I think his first responsibility is to the people, the ones who give him all his material . . . and he gives them back, we would hope, some little more insight and perception. But I just write it down as I see it. I love to think that I'm coolly objective, but I've no doubt that if you look at some of my stuff, it's outrageously weighted on the side of the bottom dog. So in a little way I help. But never forget what Auden said – and I think he's right – that he doubted whether writing one extra poem, or short story, ever went even a part of the distance to solving a major problem. So I don't believe in agitprop. What I do believe in is sensible writing about things that count. And I think there are great big gaps – it appalls me that there has never been a novel about life in a motor car factory. I'd love to see it. I say to myself in the meantime that I can't wait for the ideal socialist state to come. I've got to record as well, and I try to do that.

Q: Are you conscious of writing for any particular audience?

SC: It's just the same as when I started. A message in a bottle. But *The Thin Seam* was perhaps an exception, because I knew some of it would only be understood by the lads. It was too technical, too uncompromising. It was *read* by the lads as well. One miner wrote to me and said that he'd worn seven copies out!

Q: *The Thin Seam* was obviously a little experimental. How conscious were you of this?

SC: One had to experiment with dialect, just how one could flavour the writing with the right words. . . . But the trouble with *The Thin Seam* is that it makes no concessions. It could do with expanding a bit – too many strange words, out of context, is one of its main faults. But I like the writing there, and I'd like to do some more writing of that kind – clipped, elliptical writing – because that's pretty near working-class speech.

Q: Can we finish by asking you about television drama. What attracted you to writing for television?

SC: Well, I think the first thing I did was a commentary for a film which just missed winning an award, *A Month of Sundays*, about Shotton Colliery. It was a marvellous film but we went back and nobody spoke to us. In fact, they believed, at the time, that the film was being made as a record because the pit was being closed. And it closed a month after. We didn't know, and they said we did. The Secretary was on picket duty because the strike came just after the pit closed, and they were still bringing the material out of the pit. He got out of his car and he says, 'I don't want to see your bloody faces any more. Bugger off!' So we buggered off. I have to say that without the director I could never have managed it, because this technique of writing words to fit the time and to fit the pictures seemed very complicated to me. I had an awful time, but thanks to the director we got it done.

With *When The Boat Comes In*, they came along with the usual procedure, you know, when a television producer comes in. This time he was accompanied by James Mitchell, whom I'd met before, and Alex Glasgow. They said they wanted to do this series about South Shields – the title would be *When The Boat Comes In*. So I started getting reference books out, and all the stuff on South Shields. But the producer said, 'We don't want your advice on research, we want you to write for us'. So I wrote for them, and that was my first shot. I wrote two episodes. And then two for another series called *Funny Man*.

Both writing for the theatre and for television I like very much because you're working with other people. You get out of loneliness. I understood I was lucky with my producers. The whole set-up fascinated me and I really enjoyed it, and I'd like to do more. Only it's time-consuming. It takes me about two months to do a 60 minute piece, whereas I suppose Alan Plater would do one of his sequences of *The Stars Look Down* in about a fortnight. So it's very wasteful. I suppose if I worked hard enough I'd get better as time went on. But I'm interested in too many things. Anyway I want to write novels and short stories. Above all I want to go on with my recording.

Notes on Contributors

Deirdre Burton is Lecturer in English Language and Literature at the University of Birmingham. Her current teaching and research interests focus on women and literature, metaphor, critical theory and philosophy of science. She has written *Dialogue and Discourse* (London, Routledge and Kegan Paul, 1980), and, with R.A. Carter, eds., *Language Study and Literary Text* (London, Edward Arnold, 1982).

David Craig was born in Aberdeen in 1932 and lives in Cumbria. He teaches Creative Writing at Lancaster University. His main activities are climbing and writing. He has a daughter and three sons. He has published a novel, *The Rebels and the Hostage* (with Nigel Gray, Journeyman, 1978), and three books of criticism, as well as editing three texts for Penguin and two anthologies for East German publishers. He has also helped to make two television films (Granada and BBC-2).

Tony Davies teaches English literature at the University of Birmingham. He has written on critical theory, popular fiction and the teaching of English, is co-author of the forthcoming *Politics of Reading and Writing* and is on the editorial board of *Formations*.

Jeremy Hawthorn is Professor of Modern British Literature at the University of Trondheim, Norway. He has written books on literary theory, Virginia Woolf, and Joseph Conrad, and has edited Conrad's *Under Western Eyes* for the World's Classics series. His most recent book was *Multiple Personality and the Disintegration of Literary Character* (London, Edward Arnold, 1983).

Graham Holderness has held academic posts in the Open University and the English Department, University College of Swansea. He is currently Tutor in Literature in Swansea's Department of Adult Education. He is the author of *D.H. Lawrence: History, Ideology and Fiction* (Dublin, Gill and Macmillan, 1982) and of *Shakespeare's History* (Dublin, Gill and Macmillan, 1984). He has also written articles on Mark Rutherford, D.H. Lawrence, Dickens, Tolstoi, Shakespeare, John Cornford and Conrad.

Graham Martin is Professor of Literature in the Open University. His most recent work (jointly edited with Douglas Jefferson) is *The Uses of Fiction: Essays on the Modern Novel in Honour of Arnold Kettle* (Milton Keynes, Open Univ. Press, 1982).

Peter Miles is a lecturer in English at Saint David's University College, Lampeter. He is reviews editor of the *Powys Review*, and has recently co-edited Wilkie Collins's *The Woman in White* and Anthony Trollope's *Framley Parsonage*. He has also published studies of Smollett and Evelyn Waugh.

Michael Pickering is Senior Lecturer in Communication Studies at Sunderland Polytechnic. He is author of *Village Song and Culture* (London, Croom Helm, 1982), which won the 1983 Katherine Briggs Memorial Award. He teaches cultural and mass-media studies, and his research interests lie in the social history and sociology of popular culture.

Kevin Robins is Senior Lecturer in Communication Studies at Sunderland Polytechnic. He is the co-author of *One-Dimensional Marxism: Althusser and the Politics of Culture*. He teaches media sociology and his research interests are in the sociology of information technology.

Ruth Sherry is Senior Lecturer in English at the University of Trondheim in Norway. She has been visiting lecturer at Trinity College, Dublin, and Senior Fellow at the Institute of Irish Studies, Queen's University, Belfast. She has written several articles on Frank O'Connor and has edited his plays *The Invincibles* and *Moses' Rock*. She has also written on Margaret Drabble and Robert Lowell. She holds a PhD from Brown University, Providence, Rhode Island.

Roger Webster is Senior Lecturer in English at Liverpool Polytechnic. His doctoral thesis was on the novels of Thomas Hardy, and his present interests are nineteenth- and twentieth-century fiction, the literature of the 1930s, and literary theory.

Indexes

Name Index

Subject Index

alienation: Brierley depicts, 26–7; in Barry Hines, 30; in *Love on the Dole*, 56

articulacy, ix; *see also* silence

books, as political weapons, 9; *see also* didacticism; working-class novel, the

borrowing, and dissemination. of books, 4–5

bourgeoisie: and act of reading, 4; and depiction of workers, 21–3, 31–2; and novel form, 50–1, 130; *see also* class; working-class novel, the

capitalism, 20, 130; *see also* Marxism; socialism

Chartism, 111

class: and novel-writing, vii–viii; Lawrence and, ix, 66–72; writers and, 99–100; *see also* working-class novel, the

coal mining, 20–32; *see also* miners

Communism, 29, 39, 43–4, 108; *see also* Marxism; socialism

didacticism: and critical reaction, 6–7; Tressell and, 11, 16–17; *see also* naturalism; propaganda; realism

Fabianism, 9; *see also* socialism

feminism: and interpretation of *A Scots Quair*, 35–46; Common and, 85n; *see also* women

identity, 36–9, 78

ideology, 61; *see also* didacticism; propaganda

intention, and meaning, 40

Irish writing: women in, viii–ix, 120; working-class in, 113–23

labour: as shaping force, 20; depiction of, 24, 56–7, 83

language: Jones's use of, 28–9; in Greenwood, 53–4; *see also* realism

leisure, viii, 83–4

literacy, viii

literary establishment: and Tressell, 1; and *Love on the Dole*, 49; Chaplin and, 145–6; *see also* bourgeoisie

Marxism, 29, 40, 45, 129, 134; *see also* Communism; socialism

militancy, 20; *see also* propaganda

miners, in fiction, 19–32

naturalism: in Tressell, 6; and form, 7; Lawrence and, 24–5; Brierley and, 25–7; in Hines, 100; *see also* alienation; realism

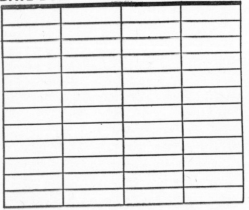